ALEX *and* PRINCESS MOMMY

Lynn Uzelac

Fulton Books
Meadville, PA

Published by Fulton Books 2023

ISBN 979-8-88982-226-4 (paperback)
ISBN 979-8-88982-228-8 (digital)

Printed in the United States of America

INTRODUCTION

Let me introduce you to Alex Isaiah Uzelac. He is sweet, kind, genuine, funny, intelligent, and simply amazing. He has no filter. When he loves, it is so sincere and with his entire heart. He will not hesitate to tell you that you have a booger hanging out of your nose or that his body is having functional issues. He loves Legos…I mean really obsessively fucking loves them. We watch *The Simpsons*'s entire thirty-four seasons regularly. Alex has autism, but that doesn't limit or define him. Autism is not a handicap in our house. We have decided to write a book all about him and his adventures. Why? To share with the world how Alex goes through life; that includes his triumphs and struggles. Buckle up; it's one hell of a ride.

I always get asked why Alex calls me princess mommy. Alex was nonverbal until he was three years old. When I say nonverbal, I mean nothing. The first time he verbally formed a sentence he was four years old. We were at Walmart, and he asked for a video game. I will never forget that moment. He pointed and gestured for a *Mario* and *Princess Peach* game. I told him yes, and he looked me right in the eyes and said, "Thanks, my princess mommy." I was so, like, "holy shit." And it just stuck. Here he is, about to be eighteen years old, and I am still his princess mommy.

Let me tell you a little bit about this journey. First, I swear a lot. I am fierce, passionate, and protective of all my kids—but especially Alex. I believe in encouraging him to always try new things, to put himself beyond his comfort zone, and to love life. From a very young age, I have always told Alex that the world will not adjust to him. He needs to learn to adapt to the world. He has every right to be here and enjoy life just like everyone else. I am especially his advocate when it comes to this. Next, I am far from the "perfect" parent. I am untraditional in that sense. I am a hot mess day in and out. Some parents desperately want that perfect-parent persona. Fuck that. Nope, not me and my house. This does not cover the traditional educational information, facts, and statistics. You can google that. I would recommend using Autism Speaks, CDC, and/or National Center for Autism for credible information. Finally, this does not have the "poor me" vibe and feelings. Yes, Alex has autism. Yes, he has challenges. But it is not the end of the world, and he does not have some terrible terminal disease. So there is no pity party here.

The Diagnosis

I knew my child was different. I knew when he was one year old that something wasn't right. He was born on April 26, 2005, and was about a month early. Within that first year of life, he was in the hospital for pneumonia (twice), RSV, influenza, and shigella and had a handful of ear infections. He was always sick. But he hit all his developmental milestones. That was until shortly after he turned one. He lost all of his speech, only liked to line his toys up, would not engage in social playing, avoided eye contact, and did not want any form of physical touch. The only time he tolerated me hugging and holding him was when he was sick. What happened? Now before I proceed to tell you about the weeks leading up to this, I just want to say I am not an anti-vaxxer. I believe and support science and believe that vaccines are there to protect the at-risk populations.

When he was around sixteen months old, Alex got five vaccines at his doctor's visit. He was behind due to being sick in that first year. His pediatrician reassured me it was safe to give so many at once. So we did. Within an hour, he developed hives. I took him to the local emergency department, and he was admitted for allergic reaction and pneumonia. He was hypoxic and spent five days in the peds unit before being discharged. Slowly over the next one to two months, he began to regress. Did the vaccines give him autism? No. Autism is genetic. I believe it is similar to a light switch and can be "turned on" by certain environmental factors. If it wasn't the vaccine that triggered it, then it could have been the next infection or fever.

At first, his pediatrician was not concerned with the developmental regression. He said it was because of all the illnesses Alex had during that first year or so of life. He theorized that Alex simply didn't want to talk or that his older brother and/or other family members must be talking for him. At this time, autism was not widely spoken about or accepted by most parents. And I get it, no one wants to hear that there is something "wrong" with their child. I began to do some of my own research. It made so much sense to me. Alex was regressing even more, and at his next appointment, I asked the pediatrician if Alex could be autistic. I again was reassured that he was a normal little boy and that I was just comparing my boys at similar ages. I was told that I was worrying too much and that regression at this age can be normal. Okay, I guess that could be. His oldest brother, Nickolas, was two years older, so I suppose I was comparing behavior between the two of them. But then his behavior became even more odd. He started to avoid eye contact, to move and flap his hands when he wanted something, and to sought after visual stimulation.

One fall day, he literally looked outside at the tree limbs blowing in the wind, causing the leaves to fall. He was mesmerized by this, and for hours, he didn't move from the windowsill. He would not functionally speak except for saying "ducka, ducka" or screaming. He craved hitting his head on things. He no longer would interact with his brother and play. He loved to spin in circles, and then he would blow bubbles. And he stopped sleeping, like he seriously would only sleep for two hours a night with maybe one thirty-minute catnap during the day. Over the next six months, I asked several times for Alex to be evaluated for autism and other developmental delay conditions. Again, I was reassured he was "just fine."

I was starting to feel crazy. I know my son, and his behaviors were just getting more bizarre and more frequent. I was a young mother, studying to get into nursing school. The pediatrician seemed very annoyed with me: how dare I kept questioning him.

We found a new pediatrician. At the first visit in August 2007, the pediatrician walked in and spent maybe five minutes in the room with us before asking me if Alex has autism. I started crying because finally a medical professional was listening to me and completely agreed that Alex's behavior was not normal. The pediatrician's office started the referral process, which would take months. I started my own research and came up with a plan.

On October 15, 2007, Alex was diagnosed with having severe autism, OCD, and sensory processing disorder. I was told that he would need to live in a group home when he is older, that he would never be able to feel or show love, that he may never talk, that he probably has some mental retardation along with autism, and that he would not be functional in our society. It was hard to hear. So fucking hard. It was bittersweet. A part of me was angry. I was angry at how much time had gone by since he initially started showing signs of having autism. I was angry that the first pediatrician kept blowing me off and gaslighting me. I was not angry with the diagnosis but was angry with their "expert" prognosis. How can these specialists tell me these things about my son who they had met for two hours? They said we had until about the age of eight to see where his functional level would be projected as an adult. I hated what they were saying. But I was so glad and relieved that we finally had a diagnosis for what was going on. For the insurance to pay for therapies, you must have a qualifying diagnosis. So now we could start an intensive therapy regiment including psychiatry, psychology, behavioral, OT, PT, and speech therapy. I cried the entire hour-long ride home from Iowa City. I told myself, *I can cry today, but then it is time to get to work. I will not feel sorry for myself or Alex. He doesn't have cancer or some terminal condition. He is not going to die because he has autism. We can do this.* I also promised Alex that I would always advocate for him—always. Never will I settle for an answer that I knew in my gut was wrong. I will fight and advocate for him and for what is in his best interest.

What Is Austim?

Here is a basic overview of what autism is because let's be honest, you can google this. Autism spectrum disorder is a neurological developmental disability that can impair the ability to communicate and interact with others. Autism has deficits in social communication and interaction. Restricted, repetitive behaviors and/or interests are common. These symptoms appear early in a child's development. Children at a young age can have very little interest in social interaction, lack eye contact, use absent or limited atypical gestures, inappropriate play with toys, and loss of language.

Holy shit! My Alex engaged in every single one of these behaviors. Alex would just line up his toys, especially cars and trucks. He was so confused and would get angry when we would show him how to actually play with them. Alex would also grab my hand to open doors, with his hand on top of mine. He loved to grab and watch sand fall through his fingers. Alex would communicate and/or socialize very little, like as little as possible. He had amazing gross motor skills, as he could run and climb. But he severely lacked fine motor skills. As he got older, he did not understand jokes and sarcasm. This is still an issue that we work on today.

Early diagnosis and using interventional tools such as intensive speech, occupational, behavioral therapy, music therapy, and food therapy can directly contribute to the child's functionality. Basically, the earlier you start therapy, the better the prognosis. And I can't tell you how detrimental it is that everyone is on the same page. This means every person who will be regularly involved in the child's life at home, school, day care, church, or anywhere else must all be on board.

Now What?

In the beginning, I felt so overwhelmed. Where do I start? All the research I had done supported getting as much therapy as possible. I read everything and anything I could get my hands on about autism. The problem with this is that the insurance company only wanted to pay for one session a week of OT and speech. Are you fucking kidding me? That is not enough. All the literature recommended speech and OT both two to three times per week. I printed off my insurance policy manual and became a coding specialist. With the help of his new pediatrician, we were able to get insurance to pay for speech therapy and OT two times a week, behavioral therapy two times a month, and PT once a week. We paid out of pocket for the additional session of speech therapy and OT every week. I worked as a waitress while going to school full time. I would pick up extra shifts to pay for it. We made too much money for a medical card to help out. Alex's dad, Nick, joined the army in later 2007. A big reason why was for the insurance for Alex. I learned and became a certified in ABA therapy, and I based how we interacted with Alex off this. We made communication boards and sensory boxes and had swings/spinner boards made for vestibular therapy. Alex was hyposensitive to stimuli while at home but was definitely hypersensitive out in public. We had a bag that we would take everywhere that had noise-cancellation earmuffs, sunglasses, gloves, and hat. I had a routine, and he thrived with it. I worked with him individually for two hours each day every day no matter how tired I was from work, school, and being a mother. I made sure everyone who was going to be a staple in his life was on the same page. My parents, sister, and best friends made up our special support group.

Let's talk medications. That is an important tool that really helped Alex. There is such a taboo still in our society about medicating children with psychiatric drugs. At first, we were resistant to try any pharmaceutical medications. I thought to myself, *If someone needs to use a walker, it makes it so, then they can do things that they previously couldn't—but safely.* I compared this with trying to use medications. So I agreed with his child mental health provider to try a very small dose of Risperdal when he was four years old. Along with the therapies and coping skills, the medication helped to curb his severe social anxiety and OCD. It seemed to be working well but then *boom!* He developed gynecomastia, so we had to discontinue. From there, we added Prozac and BuSpar. Later, when he hit puberty, which was a bitch, we had to add Haldol and Abilify to help with how violent his meltdowns were becoming. I am not promoting any medication regiment; this is just what worked for Alex. It was like night and day with going out in public. Alex previously would get so overstimulated that even a simple and quick try to the grocery store usually was cut short due to having a meltdown. We were starting to be a prison in our own home; I refused to just keep him. Medications greatly helped to be able to safely leave the house and venture out into the world.

We tried diet modifications: no gluten or casein diet and no red food dyes. We did see some improvement, but I am not sure if it was from the diet or more from the extensive therapy. Maybe a combination. We tried music, food, animal, and group therapy also. Alex was not a fan of any of those. Alex ate the same foods every day from the ages of two to five years old: corn, grapes, watermelon, chicken nuggets, Oscar Mayer hot dogs, and french fries. He had sensory problems even with his food. He would smell his food before eating it. If the hog dog was not an Oscar Mayer one, he knew and wouldn't eat it. All his senses were so heightened. Another example is that we had to avoid certain stores who used the LED lights. Not only was he sensitive to the light but also to the very soft buzzing sound they gave off.

The hard work was paying off. Alex began to emerge from his shell. We were all on the same page with Alex, and it was a painstakingly slow process. We approached meeting Alex's needs in phases and would require more from him at each phase. At first, if Alex wanted something, we would settle for him pointing at what he wanted. When he mastered that, then we would require him to have eye contact and for him to point at what he wanted. When he mastered that, then he would need to make eye contact, point, and try to verbalized what he wanted. This last phase was the hardest phase for him to master. But we all stuck together, so there was no weak link. I did try a couple support groups, but honestly, they were terrible. They were a bunch of whiny people who wanted the world to feel sorry for them that their child had autism. I remember in one of the meetings a woman was crying because her child was diagnosed a couple months ago. I asked her what had she done to help her son. I was told basically bare minimal because "it was too hard." I asked about diet modification, ABA, and different therapy regiments. But all that was too hard. It was much easier to cry about how unfortunate you were to have a kid with autism. I reminded her, and the rest of the group, that her child had autism. They didn't have a terminal condition, so stop acting like it. I was not a fan favorite there. That was perfectly fine with me; they were not my kind of people.

We went back a year later for Alex's follow-up visit at The University of Iowa. To say they were blown away by his progress was an understatement. They kept saying, "This can't be the same kid." He was talking, making eye contact, and having some brief moments of social engagement. But the craziest thing they realized was that he definitely did not have any mental retardation, and it was actually just the opposite. At three years old, he could read and write with his dry-erase board. He was so highly intelligent.

Over the next two years, we just kept with it. He went to pre-school when he was four years old to help with socializing. He was at a private preschool, and they did not have the resources to keep him safe. So my mom went to preschool with him twice a week for a year. She also got him to therapy when I needed help. I was in nursing school full time, and my husband was deployed on his first deployment to Afghanistan. She was my saving grace, and honestly, I could not have done it without her.

By five years old, Alex was talking like crazy. He had been diagnosed with hyperlexia and was a savant for his photographic memory. If he read or see something once, then it is forever in his memory. This kid was so smart, and his funny personality was really coming out. I have to give a shout-out to his brother, Nickolas. He had always been so kind, patient, and caring with Alex. Alex got more attention because, well, he needed more attention than Nickolas.

Alex was now getting ready to go to school. How were we going to navigate through this? The first IEP meeting did not go well and ended with my telling the superintendent to fuck off. I had read the Illinois IEP guide and was ready to advocate for Alex to have an education in a safe environment. You wanna fuck around with me and literally tell me that it would be easiest for the teachers to just throw Alex in special ed? They were about to find out I was not an uneducated parent who would just let you do what you wanted with my child. My goal was for him to thrive in life and not hope for the bare minimum.

Onto the Memoirs

I began sharing about Alex on Facebook when he was five years old. I made the decision to share Alex with family and friends on Facebook. I decided this one day after having a coworker come up to me and tell me how sorry she was that my child was autistic. I laughed and told her how amazing Alex was and not to feel sorry for me. She looked surprised at my reaction. I then told her if she met him, she would see why I'm so lucky to be his princess mommy. Don't get me wrong, it is no picnic in the park. Some days really fucking suck and are full of meltdowns for hours. I share these moments as well as the good ones. I share his struggles and successes. I share about him in hopes that other families with autism realize that they are not alone. I share about him to educate others about autism. I share about him to promote a positive perception of autism but also show the realistic side of it. So let's get started!

ALEX AND PRINCESS MOMMY
2010 and 2011

May 2010

- Took both of the kids to the dentist. No cavities…hurray! Alex did much better this time, well, besides lying down on the floor while screaming at the top of his lungs at the dentist, "I have no teeth. I'm dead."

  Alex has always been really sensitive with brushing his teeth and haircuts. When he was little, I would literally have to hold him down to accomplish both.

- Today, my toilet broke, and water was spraying out of the top of the damn things. Water is going everywhere. I asked Alex to help me and hand me the towel. Alex looked at me and said: "Don't worry. We will fix it." He then went over and knocked on the TV, yelling for team *Umizoomi* to come help us. Needless to say, no one came to my rescue, and Alex was demanding a hot dog for all his help with this matter. For those of you with small children, you get it.

- What a day with Alex. Today, I felt defeated. He drove me crazy. Full blown meltdowns *all* day lasted for hours at a time. He engaged in throwing soy milk on the floor and down the stairs, letting the muddy dogs inside, ripping up my 2009 tax information, climbing on the stove to jump off (broke the handle), hitting his brother in the face, biting his brother on the arm, throwing my laptop, and pour-

1

ing a bottle of maple syrup in the bathtub. Ugh. Mommy loves you, Alex. But come the fuck on! Hoping for a better day tomorrow.

June 2010

- While at the store, Alex opened a bag of doughnuts while sitting inside the cart. He then proceeded to smash the doughnuts by putting his feet into the bag. Nickolas then decided to break dance while in line to check out. The cashier was confused. I told her I was picking my battles today.

- You know your priorities are much different than other moms when your alone "me time" is grocery shopping without the kids.

- Asthma attack season. Ugh, poor Alex. It really sucks to have pneumonia and persistent asthma in the summer. Steroids, breathing treatments, antibiotics, and snuggles on repeat today.

- Not having such a good night. There was a very small space in between the concrete stairs and front door. Alex was mad that it was time to come inside. As I was putting the key into the door, he slammed the screen door to my hand. There went the keys. Alex was very happy with himself. He was singing and laughing since he now got more time to play outside while we waited for Grandpa to come to our rescue. So grateful for my dad and that he will drop everything to come help me with whatever I need.

- Alex asked for noodles today. He literally eats the same foods every day consisting of chicken ramen noodles, Tyson chicken nuggets, Oscar Mayer hot dogs, french fries, corn, watermelon, and grapes. I made him noodles, and he cheered as I brought his plate to the table. "Oh, noodles, I love you so much. Come get in my belly. Get on in there," he said and then kissed the noodles on his plate. Silly boy.

July 2010

- I just got done mowing the lawn. Thankfully, I had Alex to help me. He had his bubble mower out. He would stop whenever I had to restart my mower, and I heard him over there, saying, "Come on, just start, you fucker." I'm trying to not swear so much around him.

- Today, Alex tried new foods. I couldn't believe it. He ate ribs and hot sauce. He actually ate it and wanted more!

- If I have one more person who'll try to tell me that Alex just "needs a spanking," I will lose my fucking mind. And then the next thing out of their mouth is that they are available to babysit, LOL. No fucking way. Why would you even think that it would be appropriate to physically strike a special-needs child? What the fuck is wrong with you? If you hit them, they do not connect the dots as to why they are being hurt. Their brain works differently and often have a problem with understanding cause and effect. Touch my kid and see what will happen to you.

- Alex does this thing where he will come over to me and smell my shirt several times a day, and he says, "Yep, still Princess Mommy." This has to do with stimming and is his way to cope when he starts to get anxious. I know a lot of parents get embarrassed when their child stims. Stimming includes doing these weird quirky things like smelling things, repetitive hand movements, echolalia, rhythmic speech, or repetitive sounds. This is how autistic kids cope with their surroundings and anxiety. When we are out in public, I don't give a flying fuck if someone is staring and talking shit. Mind your business, my son is working through something right now. I would much rather have him stimming than bashing his head on a wall or floor, as he is a headbanger. He has every right to be out in public just as anyone else does. And if he has to stim when he becomes overwhelmed, then that's what he is gonna do.

- Alex went today for his three-year follow-up and reevaluation autism progress. They were just blown away by how intelligent he is and with the progress he has made. IQ test is 160. That's my boy! He really is so amazing and has come so far. This is just the beginning.

August 2010

- My poor, little Alex went swimming, and he slipped on the concrete, smashing his goodies.

  Now he is crying at the pool, asking me to kiss it and make it better…not there, buddy. I gave him a hug and kiss on the cheek. He said his cheek was not what was injured.

- Alex had his yearly physical today. He refused to speak to the doctor. He wrote on his communication board, "Oh, no, shit, run away."

- Alex is in monster mode today. He is sick and not feeling well. He destroys everything I hand to him, throwing and ripping up things. He just wants to be under his blankie and to rock back and forth. So if you need us today, this is where we will be.

- Today was Alex's first day of kindergarten. Needless to say, it was a rough and an overstimulating day. He had a successful day being in a regular education classroom with a one-to-one safety aide.

This school though. They absolutely hate me, and I don't give a shit. I don't think the school knows who they are fucking with. I am a savage when it comes to my kids, especially when it comes to their safety and well-being. And I am not willing to compromise that. Besides the to-be-expected meltdowns and running away, he did great. I am so proud of him despite what the school wanted to do, which was to put this highly intelligent child into special ed since it would be easier for the teachers. Alex's therapists and doctors are all appalled at this original IEP plan. Alex needs to be challenged, and I will advocate for him and his educational rights.

- Alex was in the bathtub, and I heard him singing, "Ain't nobody dope as me. I'm just so fresh and clean." He sang it again tonight when the dog was licking the pizza off his face.

- I am sooooo tired and ready for bed. Alex, please go to sleep early for mommy, please.

- Now sleep is not one of Alex's strengths. He has only slept for three to four hours a night since he was around two years old. When he was four years old, we had a pediatric sleep study done. He goes into REM sleep very quickly and, apparently, gets all the "good sleep" his body needs. Great for him, not so much for me.

  One night, he left the house to go to the playground at 3:00 a.m. It was the summertime, and he just had his underwear on. I realized he was not in his bed and saw him running down our street. Thankfully, we lived in a little village, and the park was literally one block away. Scared the living shit out of me. My dad came over and put locks on the top of the front and back door to keep him safe the next day.

September 2010

- Just because you are at McDonalds doesn't mean you just let your kids run wild. This little boy kept following Alex around, touching him, and laughing when Alex was screaming. Now this boy was a couple years older than Alex. I would guess around seven or eight. I told the boy to stop it and leave Alex alone. He would not. I took him to his mother, and she laughed and said "okay." But not even a couple minutes later, this kid was picking on Alex again. Meanwhile, his mother was on her cell phone and didn't care that her kid was being an asshole bully. I lost my mind on her. Not my proudest parenting moment being kicked out of a McDonalds.

- I start at Trinity as an RN this month, weekend night position. People tell me all the time how it must be terrible to work every weekend. This is Alex's current schedule, and with the hubby deployed, it is all me. Plus, Nickolas has karate and basketball. I am very grateful that my mom and sister help get to the kids' places when I need help. They are my lifesaver.

    Monday: school (8:00–3:00 p.m.), speech
        therapy (4:00–5:00 p.m.), social skills
        (5:30–6:15 p.m.)
    Tuesday: school (8:00–3:00 p.m.), music
        therapy (4:00–4:30 p.m.), behavioral
        therapy (5:00–6:00 p.m., every two
        weeks)
    Wednesday: school (8:00–12:00 p.m.),
        speech therapy (1:00–2:00 p.m.), OT
        (2:00–3:00 p.m.), PT (3:00–4:00
        p.m.)
    Thursday: school (8:00–2:00 p.m.), social
        skills therapy (3:30–4:15 p.m.)

> Friday: school (8:00–2:00 p.m.), OT (3:00–4:00 p.m.), speech therapy (4:00–5:00 p.m.)

- Alex had the ENT today. After having a meltdown in the office, Alex then decided the office visit was over. He bolted out of the exam room, through the waiting room, out the door, and across the parking lot and hid inside a flower bed. Can't wait to see how it goes next week with surgery to put in tubes no. 4 and to remove his tonsils/adenoids.

- Alex finds it hilarious to dump out every dresser drawer in his room after I just put all the laundry away. I, on the other hand, do not.

- "Hey, there's that girl." This is how Alex has been greeting Grandma this week.

- I was so excited and surprised that Alex took his antibiotic this morning without fighting me. This was short-lived. He just held it in his cheeks and then came up behind me on the couch and spit it all over me. All I could do was just laugh.
  Alex: 1, Princess Mommy: 0.

October 2010

- Alex tripped over Daisy, and I heard, "Oh, shit, shit, well, shit, love you."
  Daisy is the best dog ever and does such a great job at protecting Alex. Even when he has his violent meltdowns, Daisy lies by his side.

- Dear Iowa City ophthalmologist intern, I am very sorry that Alex kicked you right in the nuts during the office visit. I am sorry it caused you to literally drop to your knees. Maybe some ice would help. I did try to warn you that he is going to go absolutely wild when you shine that bright light in his eyes. Despite my warning, you laughed and said, "I think I can handle him." Apparently not.

- Sitting here watching *Jersey Shore* because there is nothing on to watch. After watching just one episode, Alex is now bringing me PJ T-shirts and telling me it is T-shirt time.

- October 15. Today, three years ago, we were told that our child was different. We were told not to have high expectations pertaining to his social, emotional, communication, and academic performance. Well, Alex has proved that autism does not define who he is or what he is capable of. He is absolutely amazing. I am so lucky to be his princess mommy.

November 2010

- I am gonna have to give Alex an enema since it has been almost a week since he last pooped. I have the enema on the bathroom counter; he says, "Oh, no, what's gonna go on down there?" He knows the box. It is common for autistic children to have constipation due to slow GI motility. Many of them do not eat foods high in fiber and also have sensory/emotional problems with the actual act of pooping. Alex, when he was younger, would cry because a piece of him he was losing. Alex would purposely hold in his poop. It took a while to get him to understand that it is poop and not an actual part of him that he was losing.

- Alex is on a psycho rampage tonight. It is going on two hours of screaming and fighting me. I don't know what has triggered this tonight. Ugh.

   I am pretty good at knowing Alex's triggers. But then *bam!* It changes.

December 2010

- It's a rough day when your kid is having a horrible melt-down for hours. It is made even worse when he accidentally breaks your nose, breaks your glasses, gives you a black eye, and chips your front tooth. I am waiving the white flag.

- Alex is making himself fit into the claw machine prize door. Entertainment.

- Alex told Santa that he looks like diabetes is in his near future. What? Not sure where he heard this from.

January 2011

- Alex thinks at funerals they say "reeces pieces" instead of "rest in peace."

- Alex says that the expression "time flies" means that a fly is wearing a watch while flying inside an airplane. Interesting.

February 2011

- I will spare you the details of this month. I will just say it was a medication-adjustment month. So Alex was having a very hard time. We adjusted his psych medications the first week of this month because lately he had been more violent with himself. He had loss-of-consciousness concussions twice over the last two months. Hoping next month will be better. We love him so much and will do whatever we need to do.

March 2011

- I had an amazing workout. Every muscle in my body hurts. And that was just fighting with Alex giving him a haircut.

He is now crying for the loss of his hair, picking it off the floor and trying to use the glue stick to put it back on his head.

- Just signed up for the Autism Walk in Chicago this year. This is our first year participating. We are hoping to raise $1,000.

  This was an amazing event. They had sensory room stops along the walkway. Everyone was so kind and understanding. We will make this an annual thing to help raise money and awareness.

- Alex's breakfast today: hot dog, bacon, pile of ketchup, and orange juice. It is just one of those mornings and a pick-your-battle kind of day.

April 2011

- Alex loves to get DVD movie cases out and read them. He must have picked movies from the adult shelf. I looked over at his dry-erase boards on the table, and he had written the following:

  1. *Jackass 2.5 Unrated*, all the stuff we couldn't pack into number 2
  2. *Beavis and Butt-Head Do America*, Beavis cuts the chase
  3. *American Pie*

  I promise I do not let him watch these movies.

- Field trip to the zoo tomorrow with Alex. Alex keeps telling people he is going to a meat plant for his field trip.

- Alex is having a meltdown, and Nickolas says to me, "It looks like you need to get a grip on your child." Watch it, son.

May 2011

- Oh, school district, when will you learn? I am not just going to hand Alex over to you for you to decide what my child needs. Officially done with kindergarten.

- Alex is eating Nickolas's lunch for tomorrow. He is a repeat offender. He says Nickolas needs to learn to share.

June 2011

- Pull-up free with no accidents for a month!
  Now the average age of an autistic child to be fully potty-trained is eight. They want no part of it. I hid his pull-ups, and then he had a meltdown at the store a few times because I would not let him purchase more. So he tried to steal a package or two.

- Took Alex with me to my doctor appointment. When the doctor came in, Alex mean-mugged him and said, "Oh, no, it's the scary monster man. Shit, run away."

July 2011

- Iowa City educational assessment went amazing. He had a very high IQ, hyperlexia, and scored at a fourth grade level for math and spelling. They said his memory is amazing and photographic.

- Back to school-shopping. Alex says the only thing he needs for first grade is a pair of *Spongebob* gloves. I told him he is going to be cold. He came to his senses and said, "Silly me, I will actually need two pairs."

August 2011

- Me: I love you so much, Alex.
  Alex: Oh, thanks, Princess Mommy, and I love noodles so much.
  Me: What about me?
  Alex: Not today. I only have enough love for noodles and my belly button.

September 2011

- Had a rough night with Alex. He finally calmed down and fell asleep around 5:00 a.m. I leaned over to kiss his forehead and a huge goober of peanut butter and jelly fell on his head. There is no way I am going to risk waking this child. I'll deal with his confusion later.

- "Princess Mommy, you are so adorable and cute, and I love you." He knows how to just melt my heart.

  This has become his go-to line when he wants something.

- Alex was watching his favorite show right now: *Wipeout*. He was jumping around, imitating the contestants, until he jumped off the couch and landed with the splits. Now he is lying on the floor, giving his penis a pep talk. "It's okay, pee, pee, hang in there. Don't die. Princess Mommy, will kiss you."

  Oh no, I won't. We have gone over this before, Mr. Alex.

November 2011

• I am so beyond angry right now. Alex has been talking about riding the bus for weeks, and I decided that today he could ride the bus from school to home with me. This is a huge step for Alex: to be able to ride a loud and noisy bus.

Today was the day. Alex's teacher and aide were excited for him. The bus driver greeted Alex and me and said we could sit anywhere that Alex would be most comfortable. We found our seat.

Then here came this loudmouth bus monitor telling me that parents are not allowed to ride on the bus with students. I said it's not a problem and that his older brother will sit and ride with him on the short less-than-five-minute ride. This dumb bitch then proceeded to say that Alex needs to be on the "special ed bus" with kids like him. Like him? What the fuck did you just say?

Apparently, my kid is not normal enough to ride the bus with his brother. Alex has an IEP, but it does not specifically state that he has to ride a certain bus. It took everything in me to not beat the shit out of this woman.

The principal came out and did nothing and literally just stood there as all this was happening. Then he wanted me to calm down and talk to him. Fuck you. Too late because I was livid.

Now there will be a meeting with the superintendent tomorrow morning about why Alex was discriminated against. How dare you!

• We met with the superintendent today, who apologized numerous times for what happened with the bus monitor. Apology letters were being written from the bus monitor and school district. He said he has taken disciplinary action against the bus monitor and principal. Alex can also ride the bus, the same bus as his brother, any time he wants. There are no amounts of apologies that can erase what has been done. If this person would openly and very publicly discriminate against a special-needs child with his mother sitting right next to him, who knows how she acts toward these kids with no other adults present. I have to and will protect him.

ALEX AND PRINCESS MOMMY
2012 and 2013

January 2012

- Today, Alex kept calling the pulmonary resident in Iowa City Rapunzel. She had superlong blonde hair. The best part was when she was done, Alex went over and gave her a big smooch on the lips! Oh, Alex.

- Being the parent of a special-needs child definitely challenges my sobriety at times: the sleepless nights, his health and behavioral problems, and having limited help. With Alex, not just anyone can watch and calm him down. He requires so much from me. I love him so much, and it is well worth it. I have been sober off drugs for ten years. My children are why I am still sober today.

- Alex saw a commercial for Chuck E. Cheese. He has no desire to ever go somewhere with a human-sized rat. I told him maybe one day we will check it out, and he can see it is just a person inside a rat costume. Alex firmly declined and said it is much safer to just avoid it altogether.

February 2012

- Picked up Alex today from school, and once we walked out the doors, he yelled, "I'm freeee."

- Alex almost burned down the house. Every day, he has a pizza Hot Pockets at 3:30 p.m. It is one of his many quirks. He put it on a metallic paper plate, and I now have become a firefighter in my kitchen. While I am putting the fire out, Alex is freaking out because he is late to have his Hot Pockets;

  1. there are no more Hot Pockets;
  2. there is not a microwave to cook a Hot Pockets in;
  3. I am taking too long to put out the fire; and
  4. it smells like fire and plastic in here.

- Every week, Alex gives me a pep talk and says I need to really focus and get better at winning the lottery. It is apparently embarrassing to him that I have not won the Mega Millions yet. Me too, buddy. Me too.

March 2012

- This has been one of the most difficult times for our family. Nick was diagnosed with a rare genetic heart condition called noncompact cardiomyopathy. It is affecting his left ventricle. He has been admitted to the hospital. He is on a lot of medications, will have a life vest on until his heart is strong enough to have a permanent defibrillator put in, will need to have a cardiac ablation, and will eventually need a heart transplant. This diagnosis is life-changing for our entire family. He will be medically discharged from the US army. We will be going to Mayo Clinic in Minnesota. We will get the boys checked out later this month.

- We found out today that Alex also has the same heart condition as Nick. The good news is that it is not in the left ventricle. Noncompact cardiomyopathy can occur in any of the four heart chambers but is most lethal when it is in the left ventricle. We are waiting for insurance to approve him going to Mayo Clinic as well. Thankfully, Nickolas's heart is great and healthy.

April 2012

- Dear Rock Island County Parks Department,

  It is April. You know...springtime. Please unlock your bathrooms. Alex had to go to the bathroom, but your bathrooms were locked. So he climbed the top of the tire tower, wiggled off his pants, and then proceeded to take a shit. He said it was close enough to a toilet.

- Happy Autism Awareness month to my wonderful Alex. Got him his cake and *Angry Birds* toys. Alex is so special and unique and brings so much laughter and joy to our life. Even through the meltdowns, OCD, and picky sensory quirks, he teaches me so much. Love you, Alex.

June 2012

- Alex is back to staying up until 3:00 to 4:00 a.m. every night. Tonight, Nickolas fell asleep on the couch. Alex got a blanket out, covered him up, gave him a kiss, and said, "Oh, well, shit, I love you, brother." So sweet.

- Damn those Swiffer Sweeper commercials. Now I have Alex walking around, singing to people, "Who's that lady...sexy lady, real fine lady?" The cashier at Walmart has a look of concern.

July 2012

- On a boat ride on the Chicago River today, Alex keeps making siren sounds and yelling, "We're sinking straight to the bottom."

- Just when I opened my big mouth and was about to say how nice it had been that Alex hadn't run away in a while… it happened. Alex was overstimulated at the park tonight, so he ran off into the woods without any of us seeing him. Every time this happens, my heart stops until we find him. Makes me miss the days when Daisy would chase him down and keep him safe. Not on her watch! He is now at home—safe, showered, and in bed.

August 2012

- Alex made hurdles in the hallway. I discovered this at 4:00 a.m. when I tripped and fell on my way to the bathroom. Thanks, Olympics.

- My mom: Alex, are you ready for fall?
  Alex: Chubby girl season? I think so.

  He has been listening a little too close to me being excited for the fall season.

- Made Alex a new sensory box that is in a huge rubber-made tote. The big-sized one that can hold a Christmas tree filled with beans, rice, and stimming toys. Alex stripped down to his underwear and got in. He loves it.

- I hear Alex in the bathtub yelling, "Oh, no, someone pooped in the tub." Keep in mind that he is the only one in the bathtub.

- Time to start second grade. Fingers crossed for a good year.

September 2012

- Alex has my extra stethoscope and is walking around trying to listen to his penis.

- Nickolas doesn't want to share anything with Alex tonight. Alex is in a bad mood and is trying to get the dog to eat Nickolas's action figures. Brotherly love.

- Gave the dog an oatmeal bath because her skin has been really dry. After the bath, I see Alex lying on the floor, sniffing her. He says, "She smells breakfast." Fuck. I grabbed the maple brown sugar packet instead of the regular oatmeal packet. I have a sinus infection, so I can't smell anything.

October 2012

- Alex's aide is out sick for a week. Looks like I will be his aide and will go to school with him every day.

- We are not fucking with his routine because then it will take weeks to get him regulated again. Nope.

- Time to "be Mexican," as Alex calls it, and make enchiladas. Thankful that Grandma Juana used to come over to teach us how to cook Mexican food. My husband is half Mexican and makes amazing Mexican food. He developed a love for cooking from his mother and grandmother.

November 2012

- This is the third DSI video system Alex has ruined: the first one he put in the microwave and the second one he threw out the sunroof while on the highway. This time, he threw it down the stairs during a meltdown. It broke into two pieces, and then he threw those pieces into the sump pump. Why such an intense meltdown? Because he lost at *Mario Kart*.

December 2012

- I told Alex if he wasn't good, then Santa would take back all the presents. Alex responded with, "Alex will punch his heart, then Santa will poop on the deer. You lose, and Alex wins. Better luck next time, pal." He is my child.

- Alex: Princess Mommy, do you wanna be my friend? Yeah, come be my best friend.
  Me: Yes, of course, I will.
  Alex: Sucker! You can't handle this jelly *(and walks away)*.

January 2013

- Alex is in surgery for his hernia repair. Poor little guy was so pissed once he realized what was going on. He told the anesthesiologist, "This is a trap. I should not have trusted you because you are bald. I am going to escape, then punch you in the heart, and then go to McDonalds for fries." He has a very specific agenda.

- Alex tripped over the rug in the hallway and body-slammed into the wall. He was crying so I went to check on him. He yelled at me, "Princess Mommy, don't just stand there. Start kissing."

February 2013

- Pneumonia for Alex. Geez.

- Alex had immunology/ID appointment today at Iowa and was referred to a geneticist at Mayo Clinic. It was a rough five-hour visit. Alex refused to participate and talk at the visit, well, besides saying, "You are trying to kill me." Then when we were leaving, I accidently caught his lip in the coat zipper. In true Alex fashion, he started yelling, "The doctor punched me in the lip. Call the police and an ambulance. I need medical attention." He was fine and agreed that chicken nuggets would cure his issue.

- I came home from work, and Alex had a tiny Band-Aid on his finger. I asked him what happened. His response was, "Princess Mommy, it was a great and dangerous adventure. I killed a bear today." Of course, that was the only logical explanation.

- Alex had to come with me to my doctor's appointment. While in the exam room, I farted. Alex told the doctor as soon as he walked in, "That smell is Princess Mommy, not me. She farted. It was loud and smelled bad."

- Shoveled the walkways for a few elderly neighbors. Trying to teach the kids to be good people even though Alex says he has no interest in this.

March 2013

- Mayo Clinic and Iowa City has diagnosed Alex with IGM deficiency. It is a rare, genetic autoimmune disorder. That is why he gets sick so often. Thankful that the mystery is solved.

- Waiting to board the airplane. Alex tells the boarding attendant, "Come on, plane. I need to be drinking a Corona on a beach." Too many commercials.

- Layovers are terrible for Alex, especially when there are delays. Alex is having a meltdown because he thinks the plane left without him. Once I explained what a layover is, he just sits quietly for a few minutes at the terminal. He then starts to yell, "The plane is not here yet. There is probably an engine malfunction or the pilot has explosive diarrhea."

April 2013

- I don't understand how people can go out to eat and not clean up the big mess their kid made. Autism or not, I asked the waitress for a broom so Alex can sweep up the food he threw.

- Do not laugh at my kid when he is having a meltdown. I will cut you.

- Alex had a bad day at school today. He knows that if he has a bad day, then he loses his video game for the day. He said he had a note for me in his school folder. The note read:

Dear Princess Mommy,

　　Alex was nice at school and definitely did not have a bad day. Give him his video game.

From,
Ms. Jenni

- Alex keeps calling Nickolas "nasty Nick," which drives Nickolas crazy. I guess this is what happens when you fart on your brother, and then he holds a grudge.

- Alex is going to be a big brother. Not sure how he is processing things. He keeps asking if this new child will live here with us.

May 2013

- If I one more idiot asks me if I am nervous that this baby will be autistic too, I am going to punch them in the face. Alex is amazing and is much smarter than all the people asking me this.

- Alex has a sign on his door outlining every video game system he has gotten taken away this week. It is not looking good. He is just down to having a pencil and paper.

- Watching TV and a Subway commercial comes on. Alex asks, "Can I have a donkey butt and back-fat sandwich from Subway, please?" I about shit myself.

- Alex played football this season. The coach, kids, and parents were so amazing and understanding. Today was their last game. The kids on both teams let Alex "run the ball" and make a touchdown. He was so excited to get his victory nachos.

July 2013

- IEP time for Alex. I am so mean and intimidating to the staff…boo-hoo. Why? Because I asked you to do your job and teach my son in a safe environment. The superintendent told me that last school year, I made teachers cry. My response was, "Their emotional instability is not my problem. I don't know what you want me to say. You could tell her to suck it up and stop being so dramatic." The one teacher who I made cry was because she asked my opinion on how I felt she did during the school year, and I was honest. She was lazy and terrible and did have open communication with me.

- While at the movies with Alex, during the previews, he was very irritated because there was a couple of little kids behind us talking. Alex turned around and said, "Please silence your cell phones and children."

- I jokingly asked Alex for a bite of his sandwich. He literally shoved the entire sandwich that was left into his mouth.

He said, "Sorry, I would have given you a bite, but it is all gone."

August 2013

- Before bed, Alex said he was hot. So I told him to take his clothes off. I should have been more specific that underwear stays on.

- Alex spilled his popcorn and sat on a hot kernel. He then demanded to go to the hospital due to "sustaining massive burn injury" to his right buttock. He settled for a hug and Band-Aid. He made a full recovery.

- Fishing with the kids. Alex tried to eat the minnow bait. He said, "Sorry, fishy, get in my belly."

September 2013

- Lying in bed, snuggling with my sickie Alex. Pneumonia again. Long night of meds and breathing treatments.

- We have discovered that Alex has a newfound love for singing. His favorite songs right now is "Birthday Sex" and "Holy Grail." We need to be more careful what we listen to around him.

November 2013

- The OB staff here at UPT is amazing. I have to stay for a couple weeks in the hospital due to preeclampsia with Ms. Aubrey. Alex has had such a hard time being away from me and has been self-harming. He has special permission to spend the nights here with me. I really hope that I can give him all the attention he needs with a new baby coming.

- Alex keeps asking for pasta with *mirena*. He can't pronounce marinara, pasta, and birth control, what a combo!

- Alex is having a really difficult time with me being in and out of the hospital. He has been anxious, hyperstimulated, irritable, and having more meltdowns (which can last for hours). He is learning how to cope with changes, with the help of countless hours of therapy and working with him at home.

  He snuggled up with me in my bed and said he needed to sleep in my bed with me tonight since he had a really hard day. Laughingly, I said to him, "Oh, Alex, what am I going to do with you?"

  Alex smiled and said, "Princess Mommy, just love me and never leave me."

December 2013

- Baby Aubrey arrived on December seventh. Alex said she can probably live at Grandma's house.

- Alex had a meltdown for three hours today because Aubrey is a girl and not a boy.

- Alex is such a great helper. We were running low on regular *2-percent* milk. Alex decided to make more by dumping my bottles of breast milk into the gallon of regular milk. Nickolas was about to vomit as he realized what milk he just used on the cereal he ate.

ALEX AND PRINCESS MOMMY
2014 and 2015

January 2014

- Attention, Alex:

     Please stop breaking up all the deodorant and putting it in the mouthwash. It tastes terrible. I will no longer be buying mouthwash until I know you are not going to try to poison us.

     Thanks,
     Mom

- Alex didn't want to go to school today, so he dumped a whole bottle of lotion and a box of cereal in the bathtub. Seems like a *reasonable* solution.

- Alex watched *The Little Mermaid* and now refers to a fork as a dingleberry. I guess that is close enough to a dinglehopper.

- Just got the colic baby to sleep. Cue Alex playing his drum set. FML.

- Alex loves writing, like really loves to write. He goes through an entire eighty-page notebook in just a day or two. He has such an amazing photographic memory and will write out what he reads. I need to keep my medical books away from him. He wrote and drew illustrations of "egg + sperm = Aubrey."

February 2014

- A woman walked by in the store, and there was an unpleasant smell as she walked by. Alex said very loudly: "Princess Mommy, someone pooped and needs to clean their butt." And I died a little inside.

- I buckled Aubrey into her bouncer and went to the bathroom really quick. I told Alex to babysit for a minute. I came back after just a couple minutes, and she had almost wiggled out of the bouncer onto the floor. Alex was sitting next to her and said, "Alex unbuckled her. She wanted out. You're welcome. I will take a hot dog as payment. And you were gone for two minutes and twenty-three seconds, not one minute."

- It has been a long, not-very-good day for Alex at school today. His aide is trying but gets very frustrated with him lately. I had to pick him up early today because he was hurting himself and screaming. After having a meltdown for a couple hours, it was clear he was not going to be able to function today and needed to be home where he could stim.

- Gluten-free, low-sodium chips are great until Alex eats half a bag and has explosive diarrhea. "My tummy and butthole is so angry right now."

- Alex brought me my purse and said, "Princess Mommy, I need $500 cash, okay? So just give it here and drive me to Walmart. I need Legos, like a lot of Legos."

March 2014

- Just finished up in Iowa City with the pulmonologist, immunologist, and gastroenterologist. It was a long day; Alex got in the car and said, "Hurry, let's get out of here before they find out where we live." Alex was found to have a rare genetic autoimmune disorder called IGM deficiency. This explains why he is prone to infections and why he gets so sick with them. Going to set up to do IG infusion.

- Alex's prayer: "Dear God, thank you for my video games and bless my family and please bless my penis because I really like it. Amen."

- "I thought it was just a fart, but after further investigation, I am going to need a shower and new underwear."
  —Alex.

- I asked Alex what he wanted to do today. He said he wanted to go to outer space after lunch. I told him he will have to pick somewhere closer to go. He is now pouting and drawing up plans to build a rocket ship.

April 2014

- Took Alex to the dentist today. He naturally was not very happy or cooperative. When the dentist went to clean his teeth, the drill bit flew off and hit him in the shoulder. Alex then began screaming that he was shot and needed emergency medical treatment and to call 911. FYI: it barely touched his shoulder. He required a Band-Aid (there was no markings or blood) and was able to finish the visit. He made a full recovery and also got two prices. Alex told the dentist, "Don't let that happen again, butterfingers."

- Alex is so addicted to these Lego sets, and it is amazing to watch him put them together so fast. This has also helped his dexterity and fine motor skills greatly, and we are using Legos as a positive reinforcement for good behavior. But he must think I am dumb because he has made me several maps showing the directions to several stores that sell Legos. These maps have the physical directions to the store and a store map to get to the Legos. Legos are expensive. But for us, it is worth it. I have people who tell me that it is ridiculous how much money we spend yearly on Legos. However, they do not see his improvement, growth, and behavior modification. If that means I have to work extra shifts to pay for Legos, then that's what I'm gonna do.

- What does Alex call it when we get in the hot tub at the hotel? Family bath.

June 2014

- School is out for the summer. Alex will have a new aide in the fall for fourth grade. I hate this school. We will see who they scrounge up. I don't think I am asking for a lot. I am asking for them to provide Alex with a one-to-one aide who can keep him safe. That's it. They don't have to teach him. I do that at home. We have our own curriculum at home, which is well-above what his grade is doing. Why do I have him even go to school? It is his right to go to public school and to be safe at school. He goes to school mainly for socialization, to learn flexibility, and to have some level of autonomy without me physically being there. It would be much easier for me to just homeschool him. But that wouldn't challenge him in those areas. The teachers, principal, and superintendent hate me because I am Alex's advocate. I will not just do whatever they want. This school has proven that Alex's best interest is not on their agenda.

I don't give a fuck who doesn't like me for advocating for Alex. I am not unreasonable with my expectations.

- Problem today: Alex insists that he works for Legoland now as a master builder and is having a meltdown because I won't drive him to Chicago Legoland to go to work. He even packed a lunch and snacks and drew out his building plans.

July 2014

- Alex has a special love for Frank's hot sauce and chicken. He came out of my room with tongs and a feather. I have a supermeganest that has been built right in my bedroom window. Alex opened a small part of the window and tried to extract a baby bird that was in there.

  Me: Alex, what are you doing?
  Alex: I'm trying to get the chicken for Daddy to cook.
  Me: Alex, those are baby birds, not chickens.
  Alex: So are we going to eat the tiny chickens or not? I have my red-hot sauce. My belly is ready.
  Me: No, no, we are not. LOL.

- Nick is back in the hospital for his heart problems. Alex doesn't like his homelife routine changes. Stimming all night.

- I told Alex that we were out of corn for dinner. He had a meltdown over it. After an hour, he calmed down. Tonight is family movie night, so I was going to make popcorn. He took a bunch of popcorn kernels and filled up the bathroom sink with them. He also added in two tubes of toothpaste.

  Me: Alex, why would you do this?

Alex: Leave it alone. I am growing corn and maybe a bean-stalk. *SpongeBob* and *Halo* guy will watch it overnight. And you can't have any when it's real corn.

August 2014

- Today was Alex's IEP meeting for fourth grade. I was running late, but Nick got there on time. He said everyone looked so happy when he told them that I wouldn't be there. One teacher said to him, "Oh, so Lynn is not coming then today?" Their happiness was shattered when he told them I was just running late. The bitch is on the way! Ha ha ha! I must say that I do like this new aide. She is an actual teacher, and Alex seems to like her too. Hopefully, this Ms. Rhonda will be the one. We will see. It is easy to just fall in love with Alex. It is much more difficult to handle him during a meltdown.

- Aubrey is teething. Aubrey wanted to sit with Alex. He was not happy and told me to get my child before she got acid slime (aka drool) on him.

- Random fact of the night by Alex: "Mom, I know about it, and everyone has a hole in their butt for farts to come out."

September 2014

- I don't know why but Alex hates Mexican music. When Nick misses his mom or grandma, he plays it in the car or while cooking. Nick turned it on today, and Alex was yelling, "Oh, no, the Mexicans are coming." Even though I tell Alex that he is part Mexican, he says he doesn't believe it. He is not racist. He just hates their music, so anything associated with it, he just isn't a fan of.

- When Alex gets a loose tooth, he will stop at nothing to get it out. Sometimes, it really sucks that he doesn't feel pain like others do, especially when he is trying to sneak pliers in his room to get the tooth out.

- Aubrey accidentally smacked herself in the face with a book and started crying. Alex actually gave her a hug tonight. This is huge progress for Alex. Granted, the hug was very brief and involved very little physical contact (as if she was on fire), but it was still a hug. Alex has sensory processing disorder and can have a meltdown when overstimulated by things like physical touch. That is why he is not fond of hugs. I don't make him give hugs to people. You can ask him, but if he doesn't want to hug you, then that is it. This goes for all my children. I don't care who you are, family or not. If my child doesn't want to be touched/hugged, then don't you dare try to force them.

October 2014

- Alex stumbled out of his bed and came into my room. Still asleep, he told me, "Princess Mommy, I am bringing booty back because I know about it." Then went back to sleep.

- Just got done with Alex having a meltdown for two hours because the dog ate one of his chicken nuggets. He wrote the dog a very strongly worded letter afterward.

- I went up to school because Alex was having a really bad day. Alex is adjusting to his new aide and to fourth grade, but it takes time. He hates change. I got there and gave Alex his emergency anxiety medication because he was hurting himself by head banging. I asked him what was going on. He said, "Well, Princess Mommy, my eye hurts. I'm sick. I can't walk. I hate this pencil. The clock on the wall in art class was just too loud. I have hiccups *(he then hiccupped once).* My neck is broken, and I had a stroke *(as he dramatically twists his neck to the left and sticks out his tongue to show me his stroke).* So let's just go home so I can build Legos, and we will try school again tomorrow." I really had to hold in my laughter and got my shit together. I really hope he does not scare off his new aide because I really like Rhonda. She has been really good and patient with him and agrees with setting boundaries.

- Trick-or-treating tonight and Alex only wants to collect two pieces of candy and a chicken sandwich.

November 2014

- At the muscular neurologist with Alex in Iowa City. When the doctor asked Alex to see how strong his leg muscles are, he told him, "No, thanks, pal. I have a strong wiener, so there's that." Wait, what?

- Yesterday, Alex picked a *Frozen* ring as his prize at therapy for having a great session. He had been trying to bribe me with this plastic ring all night. I took the ring, and in exchange, he wanted a $160 Lego set. Needless to say, a meltdown ensued. He finally passed out around 3:00 a.m. This morning, before he left for school, he told me that he would be back for me, that he loved me, that we needed more hot sauce from the store, and that I had fat fingers. Thanks.

- Holy microwave fire. Alex, you cannot put pizza rolls in the microwave while they're still inside the plastic bag! I am putting out a fire while he is screaming because he wanted to have his pizza rolls at 3:30, and now it's 3:34, so it's "game over," and we have no more in the freezer. After the fire is put out and the microwave is still smoking outside,

I ask Alex what he learned today. "That Princess Mommy needs to buy extra backup pizza rolls from the store."

December 2014

- Alex has had a rough week at school. Yesterday, during one of his meltdowns, he was pretending to sneeze on the other kids. When asked why, "Because I will lose my video games and Legos if I hit. So I used chemical warfare." Apparently, I have been watching too much news coverage about the Ebola outbreak. He is home from school today for a mental health day. I'm sure Ms. Rhonda can use one also after this week.

- Today is Aubrey's first birthday. Every night since she came home from the hospital, Alex has asked me if she is going to stay here tonight. I tell him yes, she lives here. Tonight, he has finally accepted that. It only took a year.

- When autistic kids have their meltdowns, it is not because they are being bad. They are frustrated because they lack the verbal ability at the time to communicate what they need. For Alex, when he is overstimulated or there is a change to his routine, a meltdown can occur. This is not him acting like a brat. This is not going to be fixed with "he needs a spanking." To that statement, I always say, "So you think it is okay to physically hit a special-needs child who doesn't understand why you are even abusing them?" Get the fuck outta here.

- I don't give a fuck when people stare and give their unwanted opinions. I have been dealing with this for years, and it doesn't bother me one bit. I am focused on my child, who is mentally struggling while having this meltdown. But many parents, especially the ones who are overwhelmed with newly diagnosed kids, are very hurt by it. So the next time you are out in public and see a kid having a tough time and "acting like a brat," just remember there could be something deeper going on that you have no idea about. Going out in public and wading through meltdowns are necessary to teach them coping skills. If it bothers you, then you can always mind your own damn business.

- Alex is sitting in the living room in his underwear. He says Dad and Nickolas will be in their underwear soon too, and that it is underwear day for the men. "We are doing like so much man stuff today, Princess Mommy."

- I am so proud of Nickolas and the young man he has become. He is so good with Alex. It is not easy to have a sibling who always has the attention and requires too much of my attention. But he loves and understands Alex. When Alex has bad meltdowns at school, they will go get Nickolas out of his class until I can get there. He has an unbreakable bond with him.

- As a test, I put some presents under the tree for the kids to open on Christmas Eve. Alex lasted not even one day before breaking down and opening all of them. Before this opening frenzy occurred, he made a video on his iPad and wrote me a letter stating why these presents must be opened. It reads as follows:

Dear Princess Mommy,

I know there are Legos in here. I know it. I need to open them. I cannot control myself or my hands. Do not be mad, as you know Legos are my ultimate weakness. I will open Nickolas's presents too. It is okay because you can just buy more presents for under the tree, and I will probably open

35

those too. You can just keep replacing them. And, Mommy, we need more Franks RedHot sauce.

Love,
Alex

January 2015

- Aubrey keeps walking around, asking for a "man, man" (her way of saying snowman). Alex is annoyed by this and says "here is a man, man for you" and gives her a *Halo* action figure.

- Alex asked to use my phone to play a game app on it. Instead, he successfully ordered $824 worth of Legos. My phone automatically saved my login and payment information. This was changed today. My sneaky boy!

- Went to a Chicago Blackhawks hockey game tonight. It was a rough time for Alex. He was confident he would be okay with the noise and lights. At first, he was upset that he couldn't have an "ice-cold, genuine draft Bud Light," as he had seen in the commercials. It only went downhill from there. It was supercrowded, which led to people touching him, which he did not tolerate. He and I spent the entire game sitting in the stairwell. The stairwell echoed, and there was hardly any other noises. Even with his sunglasses and noise-cancellation earmuffs, it was just too much. It's okay; we will keep trying. I think it is so important to keep having him try new things, similar to exposure therapy. If Alex had his way, he would never try anything new. We don't know how he is going to react until he tries. Sometimes, it goes well, and other times, not so much. All we can do is keep trying.

February 2015

- Legoland Chicago knows us well.

- I yelled, "Come here so I can change your butt." I was obviously yelling for Aubrey. Alex came over and said, "Well, this is weird. But I'm a big boy, nine years old. I can clean my own butt."

- If the worst parenting decision I have made is letting my kids eat hot dogs, then I'm completely okay with that. Fuck off.

- Alex takes his Lego building very seriously. Aubrey loves him so much and always wants to sit next to him. Today, he will not allow it during the building. But he tells her that his feet are cold, so she can sit on them. She is so happy to be sitting on his feet.

March 2015

- Alex: Daddy, can I have a bite of your sandwich?
  Nick: No, you already ate your food.
  Alex: Come on, pal! I just want one to five bites. That's all.
      Don't be a jerk. Share.

- Alex has been obsessed lately with cooking shows and wants to help Nick cook dinner.
      Grandma made him a Lego apron. He is confused as to why he has to wear a dress to cook.

- This is how negotiations at my house go:

  Me: Alex, wanna watch a movie with me?
  Alex: Do you have pizza?
  Me: No.

Alex: Do I have to wear pants?

Me: No.

Alex: I will accept your invitation to watch a movie with no pants on. I have clean underwear on. No unwanted surprises.

- Alex elbowed me in the face on accident. He replied, "Princess Mommy, I'm sorry. You're okay because you have strong and tough face bones. I will get you some chocolate." He knows me all too well. Chocolate will fix this.

April 2015

- Aubrey was excited to see Alex, so she ran up to give him a hug. Instead of a hug, she headbutted him right in the junk. Needless to say, Alex is not very happy right now, and he is putting Band-Aids all over his balls.

- Autism Awareness Month post:

    Every year, we celebrate Alex being "awesomely autistic" with a party and Legos. He is so amazing, intelligent, funny, and has come such a long way from being diagnosed as "nonfunctional" eight years ago. They told me that he would never feel compassion, love, or be able to care for himself. They said he may have some MR along with the severe autism diagnosis. Boy, did he prove them wrong! He is so intelligent, with a high IQ, and he has a photographic memory. It has not been easy: the countless hours of speech therapy, OT, PT, and behavioral therapy. Then there is his medical problems too. Trying both holistic and traditional Western treatments, all the hard work not just Alex has put in but our family. This includes my parents and sister who have been amazing with helping out and all of them being consistent with him, especially during my husband's two deployments. They stepped up and helped to make sure we were all on the same page with him. This was so important. Our village is small with Alex, but they are all we need.

- Alex is freaking out because he thinks the dyed eggs for Easter have baby chicks in them. I told him they don't, but he doesn't believe me. So he made a nest out of blankets and sat on the eggs. Now Aubrey is screaming because she wants the eggs, but they are all smashed. It is a fucking shit show here.

- Nickolas has one last baby tooth that needs to come out by next week or they will have to pull it. I told him I would give him $20 if he pulls it out before then. Alex is following him around the house, demanding to pull out the tooth. He states, "I need that tooth for Lego money."

May 2015

- You would not believe the complete turmoil that is happening in my house right now from having tacos on a Thursday instead of a Tuesday. Alex is not very happy.

- Shopping for a hot tub. I look over, and Alex has stripped down inside the store and is getting inside the display hot tub. Water is everywhere. I guess we will take this one and a free towel.

- At the zoo, the bear is not anywhere to be found. Alex starts to have a meltdown because he really wants to see Paddington. He brought an orange marmalade sandwich for him. I told him the bear was at the doctor. So now he thinks the bear is going to die. He keeps saying "RIP, Paddington" as he eats his sandwich.

June 2015

- Alex is very protective over his Lego building area. He is currently informing Aubrey of the rules he wrote out that she must follow, and if she doesn't comply, then she will immediately be returned to Mommy's belly. Hmm...no, thanks.

- Questions to ask your child without any prompting:

  1. What is something Mom always tells you?
     No, Alex, you only get Legos on Lego Friday. Is your butt clean?
  2. What makes Mom happy?
     When I don't eat like a cat.
  3. What makes Mom sad?
     When she has no cake or if she misses me.
  4. What was your mom like as a child?
     A tornado.
  5. What is your mom really good at?
     Snuggling me and eating chocolate.
  6. What makes you proud of your mom?
     She doesn't pee and poop outside like a bear.
  7. What do you and your mom do together?
     Eat, snuggle, and yell at Nickolas because he is nasty.
  8. How are you and your mom alike?
     We are best friends forever, and she is so adorable and cute.
  9. What does your mom like the most about your dad?
     Dad wants a boat, but Mom is the boss and says "no."

- Sitting in the living room, I asked Aubrey if she pooped in her diaper. She said "no." Alex said, "Well, if it isn't her, then it must have been me. That fart was a little squishy."

- Current situation: We are at Monkey Joe's Trampoline Park. Aubrey is screaming. Alex is demanding me to "handle your child." Thanks, Alex.

July 2015

- Alex flushed an entire package of baby wipes down the toilet. Why? Because he needed to make sure his butt was extra clean and then a few more to clean the toilet pipes. Thank God, the plumber is here.

- Conversation this morning:

  Aubrey: I love you, Alex.
  Alex: Yeah, okay.
  Me: Alex, do you have anything else you want to tell Aubrey?
  Alex: Do not touch my Lego, ever. And your diapers smell gross.

- This damn Hardee's commercial has Alex trying to use hot dogs as a condiment. I tell him "no, we don't use a hot dog like ketchup on top of your cheeseburger." He keeps saying, "But I am an American, and this is what Americans eat."

August 2015

- Nick took Alex to the dentist today. Oh, boy…how did it go, you ask? Alex told the dentist, "If you put your fingers inside my mouth, I will bite you. It's a medical condition. Good luck."

- Back to school. Time to get my *Illinois Special Needs Advocacy Handbook* out and the number for our Equip for Equality attorney. I will advocate for Alex and what he needs. If that makes me a bitch, well, too bad. How about you just do your damn job and teach my kid in a *safe* environment. Yeah…you work on you. At least we will have our Ms. Rhonda. She is an amazing one-to-one teacher for Alex.

- Alex was reading a story about a lost dog and was supposed to write a few sentences describing the dog. Alex wrote: "The dog is big and brown. The dog ran away because he is an asshole. Princess Mommy does not like asshole dogs."
Two things:

  1. Yes, I swear too much.
  2. My kid has no filter, and he is amazing.

- Autistic kids really do have a hard time with sensory overload. I know Alex sure does. However, with lots of patience and therapy, Alex can now verbalize what is bothering him most of the time. This is much better than screaming and bashing his head on something hard. He has come such a long way, and I can't tell you how proud we are of him.

September 2015

- Alex calls Kit Kat candy bar "kitty cats," which is cute and all. But the looks we get while in the grocery store when Alex yells, "Daddy, I want to eat a kitty cat," hilarious.

- We're eating at a nice Italian restaurant, and they dim the lights. Alex panics and says, "They must have not paid the electric bill." Our server assures Alex that they did pay their electric bill. Alex asks to see the proof.

- Some days, the world is just too much for Alex. Today is one of those days. Overstimulated and doesn't want to leave the house, he says, "I don't want to people today." So we will snuggle and watch movies on the couch today.

October 2015

- Alex insists on holding my hand to cross the street. He says he is keeping me safe because I need both hands to drive to the store to buy him Legos.

- Autism does not define Alex or limit what he can do. I am so lucky to be his mom. He has honestly taught me so much.

- Alex: Princess Mommy, I am wearing a costume for Halloween tomorrow to school.
  Me: Alex, you are in fifth grade now. They don't dress up or have a Halloween party.
  Alex: What is happening? I am not an adult. This should not be happening right now. Such bullshit, I have not been prepared properly for this.

- Just in case you couldn't tell what was coming next after the last post. *Mario* is going to school with Halloween cookies, brownies, full-sized candy bars, juice boxes, and goodie bags for his fifth grade class. He is bringing his own Halloween party to school.

November 2015

- The doctor asked Alex why he is here for a visit today. Alex says he is here for some general spicy chicken. The doctor is Asian. Cue my apologizing.

- Alex was at the pulmonologist, and the nurse took his blood pressure. After the machine was done, Alex very seriously said, "Oh, man, that was risky. She almost cut off my arm."

- Alex switched my umbrella out of my car. He took my big and nice one and left me his toddler-sized, zoo-animal one. He also put a note on it that said this umbrella was too small for him, so I could use it. Needless to say, I got wet—very wet.

December 2015

- Alex: Santa, can you see me like *all* the time?
  Santa: Sure can, so be good.
  Alex: So you watch me take a bath and poop?
        And just like that, our time is done with mall Santa.

- Thank you to the QC Mallards hockey team for making Alex's day! He was interviewed by the *News Channel 6* (*KWQC*) and went on a Zamboni ride. He said this is the best day of his life.

- Alex's amazing one-to-one aide/teacher, Rhonda, is leaving. This is devastating news. That school treats her like shit and pays her crap. So I do understand. But losing her is going to be terrible for Alex. She is amazing with him, and right now, she is the only one who actually gives a shit about his education at this damn school.

Alex and Princess Mommy
2016 and 2017

January 2016

- I saw a news story today about an autistic man being shot by police due to not following instructions. This breaks my heart and is a real concern for my Alex. When he is anxious or scared, he will resort to nonverbal communication. This includes yelling and screaming instead of talking, stimming, and echolalia. He also has problems with following more-than-one step directions during stressful situations. What if we are pulled over and he is asked to do multiple things at once? What if he can't follow or he doesn't understand the directions? What if he puts his hands in his pockets? Will he get shot? What if we are on a road trip and we're pulled over and he is asked to get out of the car? He is not going to get out without his blanket. What if the police take this as being noncompliant or think he has a weapon hidden in his blanket? Will he get shot? I hate to even say this, but thankfully, he looks "White" even though he is a minority. I believed the vast majority of police officers are not racist. But it is the 1 percent who are that makes me worry. I have a window decal on my car to inform the police that there may be someone with autism riding in the car. But what if they don't see it?

- Alex puts his ear to my stomach to listen to my belly make farts. He thinks it is hilarious.

45

- Okay…let's see what one-to-one aide they have lined up for Alex as we head back to school. One hour in…this guy will not make it. Nope, next.

February 2016

- Alex was upset that his pants shrank. No, Alex, those are my skinny jean leggings. Take them off.

- Alex is pounding on my bedroom door, very upset, yelling that this is an emergency. The emergency is that he is worried he will one day grow Mexican man hair. It is 3:00 a.m., and I'm going back to bed.

- My poor Alex and his anxiety. He has now started to try to pull/remove his teeth, baby or adult, when he has an anxiety attack. Picking him up from school and to the dentist to see if they can do something with this adult tooth he pulled out. He has severe anxiety and sensory impairment, and that is part of Alex being Alex. He doesn't feel pain like others. We know this, as he has had extensive medical testing. It breaks my heart. I try so hard to protect him from others and from the ignorant assholes in this world. But it is a totally different situation trying to protect him from himself.

- Addiction is part of my everyday life. I am an open book, and I am not ashamed to tell people my story. I have been sober off drugs for thirteen years. Once an addict, always an addict. I am reminded today of how far I have come and everything I have to lose if I relapse. My children need and deserve a mom who is sober. I was a drug addict for two years, homeless, at times. I met my husband because he was my dealer. We both decided to get clean when I got pregnant with my oldest child, Nickolas. We got sober. I went on to nursing school, and he joined the US army. We have built an amazing life together and could not accomplish all we have if we were not sober. It is not easy being sober; it is really hard. Alex needs so much of my attention, and I need to be sober to care for him. So, for me, I choose to be sober.

March 2016

- Another rough day for Alex. We are on the second one-to-one aide for the year, and this guy is a lazy idiot. He has no interest in engaging with Alex or even trying to calm him when he has meltdowns. His solution: to have the office call me to come up to pick him up.

  So they are teaching Alex that if he wants to go home, then all he has to do is hurt himself or have a meltdown. This has been going on for weeks now. I have decided no more. I told the school that I'd be coming up and that I would stay with Alex and his one-to-one aide at school instead.

  When I got to the school, the aide was walking to his car. Meanwhile, Alex was on the floor in the office, crying and screaming, and office staff were trying to get him to not hurt himself. This asshole then started saying how Alex didn't listen to him, how bad he was, and how this was not what he signed up for.

  I told him, "Well, you don't have to fucking worry about that anymore. You can go home and are no longer his aide. After your smart-mouthed comments, I do not trust you with him, and you two are obviously not compatible. So you can fuck off, you lazy piece of shit."

  Emergency IEP meeting is on the agenda for tomorrow morning. They will find him an appropriate safety aide. It is his legal right and is in his IEP. I can't tell you how much we miss Rhonda. I think I am going to text her and see if she likes her new job.

- Alex has had such a rough day at school that we are on day 2 of staying home, stimming. This morning, he comes into my bed and says to me, "Princess Mommy, I need you to hug and snuggle me. I don't want to hurt myself, but I am afraid that I will. I just can't calm down." So that is what I am doing today, not homework, lunch with friends, the piles of laundry, grocery shopping, cleaning, or going to my doctor appointment. Alex and I will not be leaving my bed today, just snuggling and soft tickles. Thankfully, I have an amazing husband who will handle everything else.

- Attempting to go to school today.

Alex: "I am going to fight everyone."

Well, maybe tomorrow. We have another aide lined up but haven't met her yet. Fingers crossed. He said, "Why can't my Ms. Rhonda come back? I love her." Me too, buddy. Me too.

- It has been almost three weeks, and this new aide has called into work every fucking day. She has not met Alex or myself and probably hasn't read the Alex manual because I have gotten no questions emailed/texted to me. The school just keeps making excuses from her being sick to she had to put her dog down, her mom was in a minor car accident, and about every other excuse in the book. I hope that she is not lying, but man, this is very weird. Alex has been doing amazing being at home, of course. But that is not the point. I send him to school to socialize and to navigate through the world for small bits of time without me in a safe environment. He is incredibly intelligent, and we have always kept him academically challenged.

- I have reached out to our wonderful, amazing, loving Ms. Rhonda. I think I can negotiate to get her back as his aide. If the school won't be proactive with getting her back, dammit, I will.

- Success! Got her a raise and some added perks. Alex is so happy right now. We just came from the IEP meeting, and he keeps saying, "Princess Mommy got my Rhonda back. I just love you. She is so adorable and cute."

April 2016

- At Iowa City with Alex, who is very anxious and suspicious of everything today.

  Me: Alex, do you have to pee before your next appointment?
  Alex: Why? Does the doctor want my pee? What is he going to do with it?
  Me: No, Alex, I just wanted to know if you had to use the bathroom.
  Alex: No, I will keep my pee inside me. It is mine.

- My mom made Alex an amazing weighted blanket. My mom is so kind and talented and has made many sensory processing items for not only Alex but for the local therapy center too. She is the best.

- Trying to take a nap and I am woken by Alex who has brought me my purse. "Princess Mommy, don't worry, I just need a couple things. I just need your credit card number, expiration date, and three-digit security code. Just a couple things for this $599 purchase plus tax. You just find me your credit card and then go right back to sleep. I will handle everything else."

- Alex has been back at school with his Ms. Rhonda for three weeks and not one single time has he had to come home. *Not one!* God, we love her. And I am so grateful for the amazing bond they have.

May 2016

- I can't stand people who put their own selfish needs before their children. News flash: *You cannot be a good parent while on drugs and being self-destructive.* Period. Grow the fuck up, handle your business, and take care of your kid. If you can't do this for them, then step aside while someone else raises and protects your kid.

- I absolutely hate it when people tell me "sorry" because my son has autism. This kid is fucking amazing. You don't need to feel sorry for me or for him. He has an amazing life, and he brings so much happiness and joy to mine. Some days are hard, absolutely. But the good always outweighs the bad. I have decided to share him on my Facebook a little bit more so people can see how lucky I truly am to have him.

- Alex's separation anxiety has been pretty intense lately. He is in the shower and yelling for me frantically. His emergency: he wants to hold my hand because it has been twelve minutes since he saw me last. He misses me.

May 2016

- So we bought Alex a new bed and bedframe. Alex does not like change and is pissed. He has been having a meltdown for about two hours. "Princess Mommy, I do not want this wonderful, nice large new bed. This is the worst bed ever made. I hate this lovely bed. This is Dad's bed now." We are four hours in, and the progress is Alex has sat on his bed for five minutes.

- I got an email confirming my purchase of $420 on Amazon for Legos. I asked Alex about it. His response: "How much do you know? Okay, okay. I was very sneaky and watched

Dad put in his username, password, and credit card when he was using my iPad. I was being a criminal. It's okay. Don't be mad at me. I will kiss you."

- Lately, when I tell Alex no, his response is, "But why? What have I done wrong to deserve this kind of treatment?" This was his response today when I told him he could not have four chili cheese dogs but could have one.

- Getting ready to board the airplane for our flight to California. Alex has a routine he does with every flight that includes weather check and airline background check for safety concerns and crashes. As we board, he stops at the pilot and says, "Is the plane in safe working order? We don't need plane crash today or you will surely be fired."

June 2016

- Oh, Disneyland, you are no friend of Alex. He went on one ride until his anxiety took over. He had a horrible meltdown and was yelling that "We need to escape this terrible place. I hate it here." It was really busy and loud. This turned into an asthma attack, and we had to sit inside guest services so he could have a breathing treatment and calm down. He was content with sitting in the car with me and watching movies on the iPad while everyone else went on rides for the next eight hours. This is the part of autism that really breaks my heart.

- We went to Legoland today but not to enter the park. Alex only wanted to go into the gift shop and buy an entire case of Lego Minifigures. They were very nice. Typically, they will not let a guest buy an entire case of them since it is a much sought-out item. But after telling the manager about our Disney day yesterday, she allowed it. Alex told her, "I will also take a limited-edition Lego cup and a sign with my name on it. This is the best day of my life. Princess Mommy, give her the $288 plus tax."

July 2016

- Today, I received an email from Disneyland's customer service. They gave us five free tickets to either Disneyland or Disney World for Alex to "try it again." They also gave me recommendations of low-volume times to come. As of now, Alex says absolutely not. But maybe time will heal all emotional wounds, LOL. How nice and thoughtful of Disney.

- Me: Oh, boy, I have butterfingers today.
  Alex: I want to eat butterfingers.
  Me: No, Alex, it means I keep dropping things.
  Alex: So you don't have finger candy today.
  Me: Nope, I just keep dropping things.
  Alex: Well, that is weird that you put butter on your fingers anyway.

- I start singing and dancing around to the song "It's Raining Men." Alex gets upset and says, "What! There better not be any men in my pool outside."

August 2016

- It is a wild ride and never a dull moment with my Alex. I wouldn't change him for anything. He has taught me so much about unconditional love, strength, compassion, and patience. He continues to amaze me with his progress and with his view of the world. To think that nine years ago when he was diagnosed with severe autism that he would be low functioning. They told me that he would never feel emotion, talk, or be able to function in society. Boy, did he prove them wrong! It has not been easy but so worth it.

- What do you do when you miss your grandma? You make her enchiladas. Alex says, "Okay, I am ready to be a Mexican today and make enchiladas."

September 2016

- Alex told me that I have to get up and be an adult today, which includes taking him to Walmart to get Legos.

- Me: Alex, time to get your homework done.
  Alex: Princess Mommy, I already took care of it *(laughing)*.
  Me: Bring it here so I can check it.
  Alex: No, you can't.
  At the top of the paper, he wrote that the due date is September 2017…next year.
  Me: Well, what is this?
  Alex: Oh, damn, I'm caught. Don't tell my Ms. Rhonda.

October 2016

- I had some blood work done. Alex calls the bruises "decaying spots" and is very worried if I will turn into a zombie like on *Plant vs. Zombies.*

- Me: Alex, you are such a good big brother.
  Alex: No, not really.
  Cue Aubrey pooping on the floor while trying to get her pants off to use the bathroom.
  Alex: That girl is your mess.

November 2016

- Alex's fill-in-the-blank history homework:

  1. Civilization began in *Mario World.*

2. This is located between <u>Dairy Queen</u> and <u>Rock Island</u>.
3. There, people are known for their <u>hot dogs and chili</u>.
4. They used <u>sharp marshmallows</u> to bring water to their crops.
5. The main building material was <u>sun-baked chips</u>.
6. This early civilizations consisted of <u>Mexicans</u> and <u>raccoons.</u>
7. Life in these communities centered on the right to <u>watch television</u>.
8. This was home to the <u>gross banana-fla-vored Twinkies.</u>
9. The temple schools taught <u>the Cubs how to win</u>.
10. Women had the right to <u>own people</u> and <u>play basketball</u>.
11. Powerful <u>bus drivers</u> ran the school and managed the lands.
12. The ruler united the people by setting up a <u>taco pizza.</u>

- Alex: Did Ms. Rhonda call you today?
  Me: Why?
  Alex: Oh, no reason. It is not because I was having a difficult day listening. Well, maybe.

December 2016

- Me: I feel like I have been hit by a truck.
  Alex: *(In panic)* like a big truck hit you? Was it an F-150? Semi? UPS truck? Where are you hurt? I will take care of you, Princess Mommy, well, at least until *The Simpsons* come on.

- There is a men's T-shirt at the novelty store that says, "My nickname is El Mucho Ding Dong." Alex wants it because he loves Hostess's Ding Dongs. LOL.

- Watching *Beauty and the Beast* with Aubrey. It is the part in the movie where Bell is crying because she is sad that she has to stay.

  Aubrey: Oh, no, Bell is sad.
  Me: Why is she sad?
  Aubrey: She is crying and so sad because she must be hungry.
  Alex: Just like you, Princess Mommy.

- Holy asthma attack, Alex. Winter is so hard on his lungs. His day consists of scheduled breathing treatments and steroids. No leaving the house, as it is just too cold.

January 2017

- There was a social media post circulating that showed high school kids torturing an autistic classmate. I can't bring myself to watch the entire post. I can't stop crying and am so angry. These punk-ass kids think it is okay to harm another person, and then they are so stupid that they post it online. Shame on them! And shame on their parents for not teaching them how to treat others or how to not behave like a wild fucking animal. Disgusting! This is why Alex will never be in a school setting without a one-to-one aide/teacher. I will lose my fucking mind if anyone ever hurt him. I promise you will see me on the news.

- Had Alex help me with laundry. He said to me, "Princess Mommy, I am not a laborer, and we have not discussed my salary." I about died laughing. You live here, you help with chores. Besides, it is really good PT/OT.

February 2017

- Went to Target today. Alex yelled to the people in line in front of us, "Congratulations, it is Black History Month. It's your month. I wish I was Black so I can celebrate. You made it." Cue me apologizing and explaining that he is not being sarcastic and he is not racist. He does not see color in a way that others do. He is genuinely excited that it is their month to celebrate, and he wants to celebrate with them. So we bought a cake and celebrated at home.

- Before Alex goes to school every morning, he has a routine where he comes into my bed and snuggles with me after he gets ready. He requires at least ten minutes and calls it "going back to dream." He lays down, and we snuggle while talking about how amazing of a day he is going to have and what will be for dinner. Yesterday, I forgot to wash his blankie aka cute one. I usually wash it once a week, so it smells just the way he likes it. Today, he smelled his blanket and asked me to remember to wash it today. The details he notices is so crazy to me. He is so hypersensitive with his senses. He pays attention to everything. It really makes me appreciate how hard it is for him to go through every day.

- I was just told by a teacher that it is "too much to ask" that she sent home/email me every Friday what Alex struggled with during the week. This way, we can work on it over the weekend. I told her it can be just one to two sentences on a piece of paper sent home, email, or even call me. It is lazy-ass teachers like this that give the hardworking ones a bad name. Oh, and did I mention it is in Alex's IEP? This teacher doesn't give a shit. I told her, "Okay, but I don't want to hear shit out of your mouth about his grades/projects. *Not a fucking word.*" And this is a very small school with a very small class size. So it is not that she has so many students. I had another parent tell me that she was the same way years ago when she taught her son. I guess she hates involved parents.

- Flying out for vacation and going through security. Alex is panicking and saying, "Don't worry, I have no weapons, bombs, firearms, or any kind of explosives. And I definitely do not have any liquids over three ounces." Needless to say, he was searched. Once on the plane, he is very concerned about all the suspicious noises the plane is making and asks to speak with the pilot. Lord, please let the Haldol kick in.

March 2017

- Alex just diagnosed me with "possible pusitis." He has heard me diagnose Nick with this a few times.

- We had a difficult conversation in trying to explain to Alex about holding in his farts. His response was, "Even if I say 'excuse me'? What if I don't think it will be too loud?"

  Yes, Alex, sometimes, you need to just hold it in. He was perplexed and upset.

April 2017

- Alex to the people at the back of us in the checkout line: "I am holding in my farts for you. You're welcome."

- Alex with Easter: "I will only participate if the eggs that I am hunting will have a McDonald's spicy chicken sandwich in them."

  I did buy a huge egg, and a sandwich should fit inside it. I got one for Alex and one for Grandma Betty. She may have dementia, but she gets Alex and loves him so much.

- Let's talk about stimming. This is what Alex does by vocal tics, grunting, growling, echolalia, yelling, or moving his body in a rhythmic and obsessive pattern. It is how he deals with anxiety and stressful situations. Stimming behavior is also a clue that he is overwhelmed and that he may have a meltdown if he can't get his shit together. Some of his stimming have been turned into coping mechanisms. It is a work in progress. Alex develops new stimming behaviors and new triggers, so it can be difficult sometimes to know what is setting him off. So if you see someone out in public doing any of these behaviors, then please don't stare. Also, don't give your unsolicited opinion.

May 2017

- "I just ate my grapes. They are now on their way to my butt."
  —Alex

- Driving in the car with Alex and I ask him what he wants to talk about. His response: "Well, how about silence while you drive? You know, like you close your mouth and do not speak, and we just sit here until we arrive at our destination." He is a great conversationalist if you can't tell.

June 2017

- Every time I have Alex and Aubrey in an elevator, Alex always tells her, "Don't you dare push the elevator button." In true Aubrey fashion, she always does, and then Alex has a meltdown. Story of my life right now.

- That's a wrap with sixth grade. Some of the worst and laziest teachers I have ever seen. Summer break, here we come. The only positive is that we got our Ms. Rhonda back.

July 2017

- I let Alex use my phone last night, and I noticed that my Amazon basket is empty. I will shop and put things in my basket that I am on the fence about.

  Me: Alex, did you get on my Amazon account?
  Alex: Yes, but, Princess Mommy, don't worry, I did not purchase any Legos. And I also helped you out and emptied your basket for you. You are very welcome.
  Me: You didn't empty my basket. You purchased it.

- At Walmart and Alex announces that he did not fart but that it definitely smells like someone did. There is just an older lady in the aisle with us. Alex says, "The old lady must have farted or pooped." Kill me now.

- Alex loves winning things regardless of what it is. He just won a free tanning session and a beer koozie at this street fair. Excited doesn't even begin to describe how elated he is right now.

August 2017

- I don't know where the day will take Alex, but I do know he will be fresh. He used everyone's deodorant to be on the safe side of clean.

- Alex lost his glasses, so he tried to borrow mine instead.

- What am I up to tonight? Oh, well Alex is educating me with a documentary and PowerPoint he made about the twenty-one-day incubation period of a chicken, including the excitement of the baby chicken escaping from the egg. What an exciting life I lead.

- I had surgery today, and Alex is taking such good care of me. He consulted with WebMD and states I may develop a pulmonary embolism, aspiration pneumonia, incision site dehiscence, and/or severe pain. He says, "Oh, boy, this is going to keep me up tonight."

- Alex keeps correcting Aubrey and says he would like her to call him Mr. Alex for the rest of the night. He says she needs to show her elders some respect.

September 2017

- Aunt Lori took Alex to the store and let him pick out a toy. He chose a scepter and says this now his "hitting stick for when people don't listen to me." Thanks, Lori.

- Alex's apology letter to the principal:

    I am sorry I was having a bad day and that you made it worse. I am sorry that the chair I threw did, in fact, hit you. Why were you standing there? Maybe the blame is shared. I do not like you, but Princess Mommy says I have to say sorry. You should just leave me and my Ms. Rhonda alone.

    From,
    Mr. Alex

- I jokingly said I was going to have a heart attack watching this Cubs game. Alex turns the channel, gets my stethoscope, and says I am not allowed to have a heart attack. He then starts his research. He is now educating me about the different types of heart attacks.

October 2017

- Me: Alex, how was your day at school?
  Alex: Why? What have you heard?
  Me: Nothing.
  Alex: Well, you should buy Ms. Rhonda a present.
  Me: What happened?
  Alex: Well, there was a miscommunication, and a rookie
      mistake was made. It was rough for all. Yeah, she will
      need some coffee or that grown-up grape drink.

- At Nickolas's wrestling meet, Alex is very concerned about
  the concession stand. He insists on getting in line now. The
  concession stand worker tells him they will open in thirty
  minutes, so he can come back in a little bit if he wants.
  Alex says, "Thank you, but I will stay and wait to avoid
  the opening day stampede hot dog rush. Everyone always
  wants the hot dogs."

November 2017

- Alex would like to be a US veteran so he can get freebies
  today on Veterans Day. He is very disappointed that you
  have to actually be a veteran for that. That's okay. Nick
  took him with for his free breakfast, lunch, and dinner.

- Me: Aubrey, please do not put stickers on the walls.
  Alex: Yes, and not on your private parts either. That was
      not a good situation for me.

- Alex has a new thing where he really enjoys opening things,
  and he enjoys removing labels. So I look in our pantry and
  have no idea if I am going to have tomato soup or a can of
  green beans for lunch.

- Alex is angry that Aubrey keeps referring to freckles as nipples. Alex tells her, "This can turn into a very dangerous, confusing situation."

December 2017

- Alex's new quote of the week when he doesn't like something: "Well, I don't like _____, but it's still better than Bruno Mars." His hatred for Bruno Mars music is intense.

- Alex was trying on clothes at the mall. It was hilarious when Alex was trying on a big stack of jeans and I heard him say, "Oh god, why? Why do you want me to wear these, Princess Mommy? They are just terrible." He came out in a pair of Skinnygirl jeans with flowers on the butt. They must have been left in the waiting room from the last person.

- Random Alex thought of the day as Aubrey is watching *Dora the Explorer*, "If Swiper ever tried to steal my hot sauce, I would have him arrested or hunted during hunting season. Yeah, he better not ever mess with me."

ALEX AND PRINCESS MOMMY
2018 and 2019

January 2018

- Nick is having his annual fishing trip up North with Nickolas and my dad.

  Aubrey: I can't wait to FaceTime Dad tonight to tell him I love and miss him.
  Alex: Yeah, I will tell him I miss his pork chops and having real dinner, not this stuff that you make. Ice cream is not supposed to be for dinner.

- Alex got me a box of chocolates from the store. He also took a bite out of every single one of them. I am loved.

- Our day started off rough. I asked Alex what I was going to do with him. He said, "You can love me and snuggle me." Excuse me while I cry.

- Rhonda to the rescue! Thanks for saving my butt last minute and watching both kids. You are a lifesaver!

- Tried to play a trick on Nickolas today. We told him that we bought him a 1988 beat-up Lincoln. This kid said "thank you" and "I will make it work. I am just grateful for whatever you guys get me to drive." Such a great kid.

Alex said, "It doesn't matter what kind of car you get, Nickolas. I will not be riding in the car with him. He is a crazy driver, and I choose life."

February 2018

- "Well, congratulations on your loss since you did not win. You lost and are the declared loser. That's a fine how do you do. The winner is me." This is how Alex announces that he won at the card game. We are working on it.

- Alex: Aubrey, I am your elderly. You will need to learn to respect and listen to me. You will also need to check under my bed if I ever think there are monsters underneath.
  Aubrey: *(With the most serious face)* never, Alex. And I will tell Santa if you are going to be like this.
  Alex: Oh god, no, you better not tell Santa. Okay, okay. I'll be good.

- At the doctor with Alex for a routine checkup. Alex checking in at the front desk: "I am here for a checkup, but she is not to see my wiener bush."

March 2018

- Watching Disney movies with Alex and Aubrey today. Watching *The Lion King* and the part where Simba is changing from a little lion to an adult lion is on. Aubrey says it's magic how he transformed.

- Alex *(with a look of disgust)*: Aubrey, he went through puberty and has completed the five stages of the lion cycle, leading to the adult stage. Everyone knows that, right, Princess Mommy?
  Me *(googling it)*: yeah, okay.

He is full of random facts like this and will often make me and others feel like a complete moron.

- A rare moment when Aubrey asks Alex for a hug, and Alex actually says yes. Well, he said, "Okay, but make it quick," and is hugging her like she is on fire. But it is still a hug. This sounds like something so little and small, but it's not. This is a big deal that Alex shows empathy and allows her to physically touch him. He does love her but just shows his love in different ways.

Alex: I'm all ready for school, Princess Mommy. Just getting my shoes on.
Me: You forgot your pants. You just have a T-shirt and undies on.
Alex: Oh, dear, I don't want to be cold.
Me: Well, no, being cold would suck, but you probably don't want to go to school without pants because it may be a little awkward.
Alex: Don't want to be cold, no.

He beats to the sound of his own drum.

- "Princess Mommy, at what age can I give up tying my shoes and it would be acceptable to just get Velcro? I am going to be thirteen years old, so I think it is time."

- Me: Alex, do you want any pizza rolls?
Alex: No, too dangerous. You risk severe mouth burns if you don't take the necessary precautions.
Me: First bite and I burn the shit out of my mouth. Alex and his wisdom.

- Alex wanted to eat dinner at Wendy's. There was this man behind us who smelled very strongly of weed. Alex, because he has no filter, voiced his concerns. "Princess Mommy, it

65

smells like a skunk in here." I told him to be quiet, and we ordered our food. Alex then told the cashier that he thought there might be a skunk inside the restaurant and that the man behind us smelled like he was sprayed. After ordering, the man walked by us, and Alex yelled, "Yep, it is you. You smell like the skunk. Did you get sprayed? You smell terrible and need a shower." Thankfully, the very high man was nice and thought it was hilarious. We bought his dinner.

April 2018

- When someone says how your child just needs a spanking, and that will fix up their meltdown. My response: "So your solution to a special-needs child trying to communicate and struggling to deal with life stressors is to hit them? Wow, you are a piece of shit. Fuck off and mind your own business." I am not in the fucking mood today.

- Alex was eating Doritos Blazin' hot chips dipped in red-hot fire sauce and accidentally touched his eye. Panic had set in, and he said he was permanently blind. Don't worry, about two minutes later, he made a full recovery.

- Alex is having a sleep study done. The conversation between him and the sleep tech:

  Tech: I am going to put a bunch of stickers all over.
  Alex: Oh, no. All over? OMG, like on my wiener and butt?
  Tech: No, definitely not.
  Alex: *(Cue the loudest fart I have ever heard)* sorry, I did just fart. My butthole was very nervous for a second. That is a fine how do you do.

- When you have pneumonia on your birthday, then you get a redo. Ugh. Alex has IMG deficiency, and that is why he gets sick. It is a rare autoimmune disorder. I hate it when he is sick but especially hate it when it is on his birthday.

- Random thought from Alex: Paddington the bear would definitely win in a bar fights against Winnie-the-Pooh.

- Alex is making orange marmalade sandwiches for everyone regardless if you want one or not. Diabetic? Take your insulin. Not hungry? Too bad. Allergic to oranges? Not his problem.

May 2018

- Alex will use every single bottle of shampoo/conditioner in the shower and line them all up on the side of the tub. Then I will forget, get into the shower, and then almost fall to my death. I love him.

- Alex refers to our two German shepherd puppies as "the Germans." Cue the crazy looks in Target we are getting with Alex yelling to me, "The Germans are locked up at home. Are we going to buy food for them? Or no food since they are naughty."

- There is a prisoner being seen here at the doctor's office. Alex just can't resist.

  Alex: Did you break the law and make bad choices? You probably should have listened to your mommy.

- Alex bit into a peach, and it was moldy. Alex said, "This has never happened to me eating a Subway sandwich or doughnut."

June 2018

- Alex: I think I am ready to drive the car now. I can try today.

   Me: No, you don't know how to drive. That would not be a safe situation.

   Alex: I will read the *Illinois Rules of the Road* training manual. Then I will be ready. I do have need for speed. Besides the speed limit, I will obey the other rules of the road.

   He is now on his tablet looking up the online version of the *Rules of the Road.*

- Alex: Well, Princess Mommy, that doctor visit didn't go too bad. It wasn't great, but I have had much worse visits. I think a reward visit to Target is in order.

   Me: I don't think we will be going to Target. You were screaming for someone to call the police, yelling that you have been captured, and threatened to fight the doctor.

   Alex: So it's a maybe then to Target?

- I am putting the groceries from the cart to the conveyor belt. Alex is drinking an orange soda and telling me to pick up the pace.

- Alex has a few apology letters inside his desk, just in case he needs a quick "I'm sorry" letter.

- After watching several tonsillectomy medical videos on his iPad, being reassured that his surgeon has completed all his medical training by the nursing staff, googling his surgeon's credentials, and coming to a truce about not running away, Alex is ready to get his tonsils, uvula, adenoids (again), and a soft palate repair.

- And just like that, the Vicodin kicks in, and you are dancing with your chicken nuggets. He says, "I feel so good and floaty, like even my balls are tingling and floating."

- Alex: Do you know what happened yesterday? I thought Dad farted on me. I tried to fart on him, but instead, a little bit of poop came out.

July 2018

- My grandma passed away on July fourth. Alex is actually sad, like has empathy for me because I am sad. Taking care of her the last two years alongside my mother and sister has been an honor. I am so grateful for the time I got to spend with her. I have always been close to her.

  When I was in the beginning of my sobriety, she and my pappy were there for me. They would babysit Alex and Nickolas one to two times a week so I could go to night school. Grandma was honestly like my NA sponsor. And now I just have those memories.

  She had dementia, and that really was hard. But it was so amazing when she would have a moment of clarity and would crack a joke. My grandma was fierce, opinionated, kind, and so funny. Until she died, she would still smile at me and tell me that she loved me. Some days, she knew who I was; and some days, she didn't.

  The last thing I said to her was, "Grandma, you know you're my favorite, right?"

  And her reply was, "I better be."

  I love you so much, and I will miss you more than anything.

- Alex: Princess Mommy, these cookies you made taste terrible. Something is wrong with them.
  Me: Those are dog cookies.
  Alex: Oh, man. Okay. I will be right back.

Me: Where are you going?
Alex: To give Nickolas and Dad a cookie.

• Every time I bring home eggs, Alex will ask me the following:

1. Are those fertilized or unfertilized eggs?
2. Why have you not brought me chicken embryos?
3. I am ready to be a father to chickens. If they are not good, then can we just eat them?

August 2018

• The last six things Alex googled on his iPad history:

1. Midwest tornado season
2. *Scooby-Doo* ultimate Blue-ray collection
3. How to be a good father to chickens
4. Helicopter crashes and fatality statistics
5. Is Legoland hiring master builders?
6. Does everyone shart?

• At the dentist and Alex is laughing while getting his teeth cleaned because it tickles. Then…it happens. "Sorry, guys, about the unfortunate event that is going on right now. I do, in fact, have a boner." Just another day in the life of Alex.

• Alex's new phrase of the week is "guilty pleasure." He thinks that at Chick-fil-A, they say "guilty pleasure." I told him that they are saying "my pleasure." But he doesn't think so. For example:

Me: Alex, can you hand me the ketchup?
Alex: Yes, my guilty pleasure.

August 2018

- Me: Alex, how are you so good at playing *Go Fish*?
  Alex: I cheat.
  Me: Wait, what?
  Alex: Yeah, Princess Mommy, it is very easy. You just tell the person you don't have the card they asked for. Then I win each time and get a Kit Kat. It really is very simple.

- I get out of the pool. I'm cold, and my towel is gone. Alex is inside the house and accidentally locked me out of the house. Alex comes to the back door after fifteen minutes, dry and has my towel in his hands. He said his cars needed their own towel to dry off—my towel. Makes sense.

- Alex: Princess Mommy, I have pain inside my wiener bush. He has a hernia and will need surgery soon.
  Me: Poor wiener bush, but no, I will not be kissing it to make it better.

- It is wedding season, and Alex is practicing for "the epic dance battle" that he insists on happening at every wedding reception.

- Alex and I have an hour before Nick and Aubrey will be home. He has made a list of all the stuff we will do before they get home:

  1. Snuggle for seventeen minutes.
  2. Check the local weather and discuss any concerns for five minutes.
  3. Eat snacks for eight minutes.
  4. Watch part of *Show Dogs* for fifteen minutes.
  5. Watch videos on the Internet of people hurting themselves for five minutes.

6. Watch and cheer for Alex playing *Mario Dance* for twelve minutes, followed by a breathing treatment.

- Me: Alex, dinner is ready. We are having fajitas.
  Alex: Oh, god, no. Gross! I don't want steak vaginas. Why do I have to eat this? No, I will make myself a sandwich.
  Me: *Steak fajitas, steak!*

September 2018

- Alex is running for eighth grade student council president. His campaign slogan: Vote for Alex! Princess Mommy brings great snacks!

- Can't wait to be done with this school. Thank God again for Rhonda. He will be doing homeschooling for high school. The high school can't keep him safe, and I will go batshit crazy on anyone who hurts my child.

- Alex at his pre-op appointment: His surgeon is laughing and says in over thirty years of practice, he has never heard anyone refer to their genital area as a wiener bush. And then there was the farting during the exam. "This is a minor setback and an unfortunate event involving my butthole. Awkward for you, I'm sure. Guilty pleasure."

- Me: Alex, take a nap while Nickolas drives us.
  Alex: I can't. I'm terrified and fear for my life while he is driving.

- Most of the time, we have amazing days. Other days, he ends up yelling, screaming, hurting himself, and on the floor for hours. Autism sensory overload, OCD, and anxiety. Hopefully, in an hour or two, he will be back to my happy, snuggly guy. He will probably have a concussion from the head banging and LOC he just had, but we will deal with that.

- Alex has a photographic memory, labeled as a savant for this, and has hyperlexia. He has a very high IQ. He can tell me specific details, stats, and research data. But when I ask him how school was, I get, "Today was okay. I went to class and had lunch, then came home." That is all I can ever get from him.

October 2018

- Alex: Princess Mommy, do you think I can stay by myself at home?
  Me: I don't think so. Not yet. What would you do if someone knocked on the door while you are here by yourself?
  Alex: I would tell them to go away because Princess Mommy and Dad are not home, and I am by myself. And I would see if they are going to Target so maybe they would take me too.
  Me: *No*, Alex, you cannot stay home alone.

- Alex has surgery today. He has been given his protocol Versed and Fentanyl to get him calmed down enough to go back until the surgeon came in and said it was time for Alex to take off his underwear. Alex says, "Promise me that no one here at the University of Iowa pediatric surgery unit will see my wiener. I'm not dancing for dollars. The underwear stays on." We were listening to Maroon 5 on the way to the hospital. Ha ha.

- Aubrey came to me crying that Alex told her that she has "gitis." She has had a sore throat, fever, and body aches. Alex researched her symptoms and told her she may have meningitis.

- So proud of Alex. He picked out everything to make another little boy with autism a sensory box. When Alex was little, he loved the one I made for him, and it helped so much during meltdowns. My parents also made him an indoor sensory swing. Amazing.

- "Princess Mommy, there is no bathroom for human boys, only for roosters." Again, he takes things very literal.

November 2018

- Let's talk about puberty and having autism. It is terrible. Med adjustments, hormonal, and having feelings that they cannot control or understand. He has a concussion from head banging today. He will be home all week from school, and thankfully, Rhonda will be coming over the house since we can't rely on any of his teachers to send homework. Theses lazy bitches, I tell ya.

    In the eight years Alex has gone to this school, he has only had two teachers who gave a shit about him and his education (besides Rhonda). His fourth grades teachers, Mr. J and Mrs. S. They both worked together with Rhonda and with me. We were team Alex. It didn't matter what was easiest for the school. It was what was best for Alex. That was the best behavioral and academic year Alex had. I have a reputation at this school for being a bitch. I am not being a bitch, but I am advocating for my son and what he is legally entitled to. I will not tolerate or settle for anything less.

- Aubrey: Okay, Alex, I'm going to bed. But if you need a hug, you can wake me up at any time, and I'll give you one.
  Alex: No, that won't happen.
  Aubrey: Well, what if I need a hug? Can I wake you?

Alex: Oh, no, please don't. There are more people and dogs that live here. You should just find one of them. Leave me as a last possible hug option.

- Nick is driving behind us. Alex texts him "stop following us."

- I was pulled over by police for speeding. It was just me and Alex.

Officer: Do you know why I pulled you over?
Me: I was speeding.
Alex: Princess Mommy also ran a stop sign prior to the speeding offense.
Me: Alex, be quiet.
Alex: She then failed to yield properly before getting onto the highway.
Me: Alex, I mean it. Be quiet!
Officer: You have enough on your hands. I will give you a warning.

- There was a table of older men talking and drinking coffee. Alex asked if we can "join those old timers." Thankfully, they were very nice. We were sitting at the table next to them. As they were having their conversation and laughing, so was Alex. When we left, he told them, "See ya later, hotshots."

- Here at Mayo Clinic for Alex. His dad has a very rare genetic heart condition called noncompact cardiomyopathy of the left ventricle. We found out today that Alex has trabeculations in his right atrium, which is a precursor to developing this type of cardiomyopathy. For now, we will monitor and have yearly Mayo Clinic appointments. The plan is that when he becomes an adult, he will have a PCR/DEF placed and medications when needed.

- Doorman at the hospital: Good morning? How's your day going?
  Alex: Nothing strikes fear in my terrified heart like these automatic revolving doors I am about to journey through.
  Me: We are just fine, thank you.

December 2018

- I overheard Aubrey playing doctor with her Barbies in the living room. She said, "Are you here because your vagina itches? Do you wipe front to back? You are a girl and have a vagina, so you have to wipe front to back or you will get nasty germs in there. Do you want that? No, no, you don't." Alex, with a look of disgust, picked up his toys and moved to the kitchen table. He said he had to relocate with all the girl-part-wiping talk.

- Alex is being very dramatic, yelling and screaming, "This is terrible and torturous, and I will never participate." This is his response to being asked if he could help us build a snowman.

- Store cashier asked Alex if she could help him with anything. He said, "Yes, are the elves willingly at the North Pole or are they enslaved by Santa?"

- Alex decided that today is the day he conquers his fears of tornadoes. How? By watching *Twister* while yelling at the TV, "It's not real, just fake news." Needless to say, it didn't work. He said that was a terrible idea, and he is now more terrified than ever.

- Aubrey was telling me this very long and drawn-out story about a spider named Charlie. After about ten minutes, Alex broke down and yelled, "A spider is an arachnid, not an insect. Stop calling it an insect." He is apparently a little high-strung tonight.

- Alex says if the Grinch ever tried to take his presents, then he would just uppercut him.

- I find it so entertaining to listen to Alex talk with telemarketers who call his phone. "No, don't take me the list. You can call me back in a little bit, and I can tell you all about marble racing instead of hearing you talk about life insurance."

- Holidays are hard for Alex because they are so overstimulating. Some family and friends understand, but some do not. He is not stimming to be annoying but to help with coping.

January 2019

- Me: Happy New Year, Alex!
  Alex: Happy New Year. It's a night of alcohol and nicotine for us.
  Me: What? No.

- Alex: Princess Mommy, I'm going make some dino chicken nuggets.
  Me: No, Alex, I will make them for you.
  Alex: Is it because you don't trust me? Like how I do not trust anyone who eats regular Oreos and not double-stuffed?
  Me: Well, kind of, I guess. But mainly because you have started several microwave fires.

- Alex wants to name the new fish Camel Toe. We instead agreed on Twinkie.

- Alex was getting his haircut by a very nice Asian woman. Then I heard him say, "So do you do Kung Fu? Eat sushi? Are you from Japan or China? Do you work at Osaka?" He then bowed when she was done cutting his hair. Cue my apologizing and explaining.

- With all of Alex's health problems lately, we have decided for him to be homebound for school, and his wonderful Ms. Rhonda will just come over every day. Is it unreasonable for me to expect his teachers to have Alex's lesson plan for the week to me by Monday of the week?
  Even though this seems to be common sense to the average person, his teachers at this school find this to be confusing and exhausting. For example, this week, his math teacher emailed this current week's lesson plan on Wednesday evening. It is Thursday of this week, and still no lesson plan from science, social studies, or English. And this is how it has been for the last two fucking months. These teachers honestly do not care about Alex, his education, or do not even want him to succeed. That's okay. I have made our own lesson plan, lazy assholes. I have absolutely no respect for any of them.

February 2019

- Having lunch with Alex today. Alex is playing "Life Could Be a Dream" while we are waiting for our food. An employee asks how everything is going. Alex says, "We are doing great, just loving the married life because we are best friends." I quickly correct him, "no, not married, just best friends."

- Aubrey is trying to tattle on Alex. Before she gets a word out, here is Alex yelling, "That's fake news, no way, didn't happen." He has been watching too much TV with the political ads.

- Alex was in the hallway looking inside his pants. I asked him what he was doing. "Dad said it is freezing balls outside, but my balls are nice and warm. Hairy but not frozen."

- Screams coming from the bathroom: "Oh my god, it's everywhere! My teeth are rotting." Alex accidentally used my whitening charcoal toothpaste. He thought it was chocolate-flavored toothpaste.

- When Alex gives anyone else a hug but me, it consists of half an arm sitting on their shoulder and a good sniff. It is so special though when he gives Nick a real regular hug. Nick is such an amazing, kind, and patient dad. He knows Alex shows his love differently. Alex can be so sweet and loving. I love it when other people get to see that side of him.

- Alex woke me every thirty minutes to tell me about the weather, including any possibility of "suspicious high winds." He said we don't want a tornado sneaking up on us.

- Alex just told Nickolas's girlfriend that she could spend the night, that she could even sleep downstairs in Nickolas's room, and that he would get snacks.

  Me: Fuck, no. Never. No.

- One of my German shepherds was sprayed by a skunk late last night. Alex says it is just one reason he does not like the Germans. "They always seem to find mischief and skunks."

March 2019

- Last night, Alex notified the Chinese restaurant staff, "You have a nice place to take a number 2."

- Poor Daisy has pancreatitis. Ugh. Daisy is Alex's therapy dog and has been with us since he was three years old. When he was little, she would "retrieve him" when he was a runner. When he has meltdowns, she will lay down next to him, so he would hit his head on her instead of the wall/floor. She is amazing, but she is now fourteen years old.

- The ages of two to seven were the toughest years for taking Alex out in public. There were lots of meltdowns from being overstimulated. He had come so far due to repeated exposure using learned coping skills and lots of patience. When he had a meltdown, most people would stare and make their unwanted comments about my child "being a brat" or say "that kid needs a spanking." I didn't care at the time because the only thing I was focused on was my child, who was struggling.

   I refuse to not include Alex when we go out or to just keep him home. He has every right to be out in public as anyone else. Some days, he literally cannot "do people today," and that's okay. But we try. Why? Because he will never learn how to cope in public with overstimulating situations unless he is exposed to it. It is not easy, not at all. But it is so worth it to see how far he has come.

   I remember out of all the times Alex had a meltdown out in public, only *one* person ever stopped and asked if there was anything he could help with. This was a young man, maybe in his early twenties. Alex was around three years old. I was at Walmart in the produce section when the produce water sprayers came on. Alex freaked out and was overstimulated and ran about twenty feet before I caught up with him. He threw himself down onto the ground and was trying to hit his head on the concrete floor, all while covering his ears and screaming. I was sitting on the floor restraining him so he wouldn't physically harm himself. This man in a military uniform came over and asked if he could somehow help me. I thanked him and told him we were okay and that this would pass. I told him that Alex was autistic and that he got overstimulated and had sensory processing problems. He was so kind and told me that I didn't have to explain anything to him or anyone else. He said, "You are a good mom and are taking care of your kid. You don't owe anyone an explanation." I wish I had gotten his name because I was having a really bad day, like a "I'm a terrible mom" day. He had no idea how much I needed to hear that.

Nickolas was five years old and was with me. Nickolas had always been very protective of Alex. He was obviously very upset that people were staring, and a group of kids walked by and was making fun of the situation. This man went over to Nickolas and told him, "You seem like a great big brother. Don't worry about what other people think or say. They are dumb and don't know anything." This man then waited for thirty-two minutes while I fought and wrestled Alex to get his noise-cancellation earmuffs and sunglasses on, held, rocked, and rubbed Alex's head. He was finally calm enough to get up and walk to the car. Alex had headbutted me and ended up breaking my nose. I didn't notice the bleeding and pain until we got home, and the adrenaline wore off. But I would never forget this man's act of kindness. Thank you. And to the judgmental pieces of shit who want to stare, laugh, and make comments, you can fuck off.

- When you are at the store with Alex and he tells you to not follow too close because "you are in my shot." He is recording himself finding the DVD and his adventure through Walmart. Meanwhile, he is yelling, "You're too close. Stop following me. Back it up *(with beeping sounds)*." I feel like a creeper.

- If you got a weird message from me, sorry. Alex had my phone and texted a few people. I promise I am not asking anyone to take me to Target and buy me things, especially not my boss. Thanks, Alex.

- Alex is cuddling with an egg that he believes may be an embryo. It is not; it is a regular egg. He is playing his "egg son" music and has a blanket on him to keep him warm. He tells me, "Congratulations. You are going to be a grandmother."

    We surprised Alex and bought two chicks at Farm & Fleet. We snuck them in his room and took out the egg. We have chicks. Now to keep them away from the Germans because they would be a snack for them. Alex is so happy and excited.

- Me: Alex, are you ready to go to the Bahamas?
  Alex: I have watched all of *The Pirates of the Caribbean*. I am ready.

- Day 2 of vacation and Alex is ready to go home. Vacations are hard for him, but over the years, it is getting easier. While everyone else explores, Alex and I are looking for things that are familiar back home. He was yelling in excitement because we found a Subway, and he actually hugged one of the workers. He also loved finding a DVD movie store, and we rode the bus to look at the beach. He just wanted to look at the beach and not actually get sand on himself.

- When Alex was six years old, we traveled to California, and he was screaming and fighting me so hard that security thought I was abducting him. That was the hardest travel trip Alex had ever been on. I am proud of him and his progress. Now we just have other problems with TSA, which you will read later.

April 2019

- Happy Autism Awareness Month! For our family, we are aware the other 364 days as well. But today, we celebrate this amazing, sweet, funny, unique, special guy. We focus on what he can do, and we don't limit him because of his autism. Love you, Alex.

- Me to the waitress: What kind of sauce comes with it?
  Waitress: Peanut sauce.
  Alex *(with a look of terror)*: Princess Mommy, do not get that sauce. It sounds terrible. No, you don't want penis sauce.
  Waitress: It's just made of smashed nuts.

  Cue Alex in a complete panic.

  Me to the waitress: You are not helping. We need a minute.

- Happy birthday, Grandpa! Alex said, "Poor Grandpa and his old bones. I hope they don't break when I destroy him during an epic dance battle." Apparently, Alex has plans.

- Alex calls his birthday "our anniversary of when we first met and fell in love." He's not wrong.

May 2019

- Alex named his bear Dingle Dinkle Wieny. I tried to get him to change the name, but he said it is perfect.

- We are moving. Alex has never moved in his life. He is a nervous and anxious mess, but I'm sure he will adjust. There are more programs and services for Alex in Iowa compared to Illinois. Also, I am going to be starting an in-home cosmetic spa doing Botox and facial fillers. I need a house with an actual office right off the main entrance. We found a house we love and has everything we are looking for.

- Out and about today. Alex's new greeting, "Hey there, pretty lady." He is greeting everyone like this, men included.

- Alex did it! He graduated eighth grade with his Rhonda. Fuck this school district. Now I can relax, and he will be homeschooled. The school wanted to just throw Alex where it would be most convenient for them and not what was in his best interest since day 1! Here are a few conversations I have had with the schoolteachers, principal, and/or superintendent:

    1. Telling me my child needs special ed classroom and didn't even want to let him try regular ed. They thought the regular classroom would be too challenging. Well, he is a genius so...*wrong*!
    2. Telling me that junior high math and other subjects would be "just too hard for him." *Wrong!*
    3. Being told that Alex didn't need a one-to-one aide to keep him safe. I was told that "we don't give students a one-to-one aide because of their overprotective mother." This was despite giving the school multiple notes from his specialists on his treatment team. These four specialists all stated that he self-harms and is a runner. Keep in mind that at this IEP they have never met Alex. Don't tell me that you know what is best for my son. We had to obtain an attorney from Equip for Equality in Chicago, and they were amazing. They sent a request to go to court, and we

will advocate for Alex's right to be in a safe learning environment. The school "changed their mind" and decided to give Alex a one-to-one aide a few days before our due process hearing. One week into school, the superintendent apologized to me, acknowledging that it indeed would not be safe for Alex to be at school without a one-to-one aide.

4. Having his IEP broken by teachers who refused to have open communication. Literally, I was told I was requesting too much for the teachers. I was told that asking for a one-to-two-sentence communication (anyhow they want) once a week was too much even though it was in his IEP! These lazy teachers refused, and one said that she could do what she wanted because she had been a teacher for so long.

5. Schools not liking it when you're advocating for your kid. You are considered a "difficult parent" or, in my case, a bitch. Tough. Schools have their best interest in mind. The plan that will be easier for them, cheaper for them, and/or will generate the most state money is the plan they will push. For example, I flat-out told the school that they get more money for Alex since he has a diagnosis of autism. They tried to lie and said I was incorrect. However, the Illinois IEP guide I happen to have with me says the school gets five times more for Alex compared to a "normal" child. Try me, hoe.

6. Having my child harassed by a teacher and the school acting like it is not a big deal. A teacher who demands hugs and then physically tries to hug a child who is yelling "no" is wrong. That goes with any child. After I explained to the teacher how her hugs and physical contact are inappropriate and unwelcomed, she just laughed like it was funny (sidenote: it was really hard for me to not take her outside and beat her ass). We had to threaten police involvement if she assaults my son again. Since she didn't think she did anything wrong, we had to have it put in his IEP for her to keep her grubby hands off Alex. She was weird, inappropriate, and just creepy.

So why did he stay at this school?"

1. He was too intelligent for the special ed schools in the area.
2. He would need a one-to-one aide, and private schools do not have to provide this.
3. It is his legal right to be in a safe environment at school.
4. He does have amazing classmates who encourage and support him.
5. *Rhonda.*

June 2019

- Me: Alex, you have a bat in the cave.
  Alex: What! I don't understand your reference. Is it something with my butt?

- Alex has surgery today to repair his anal fissure.

  RN: So, Alex, we will get you all closed up afterward. Don't worry, you won't feel anything. We will knock you out. Can you tell me what is being done today?

  Alex: So today you are going to close up my butthole and punch me in the face. But I won't feel anything.

  Me: Oh, boy, no.

- Alex to the lifeguard: Don't worry, I do not have any bleeding or open wounds, just a beautiful butthole. Princess Mommy said I can swim.

July 2019

- Whenever Alex has Iowa City appointment, he gets very suspicious of everyone, worried he will have to get labs done.

  Check-in nurse: Alex, you don't drink alcohol or smoke, right?

  Alex: Why? What have you heard? Am I in trouble for suspected illegal activity?

  Nurse: No, I just have to ask everyone these questions.

  Alex: Very unusual and dubious. I will not be answering anymore questions.

- Me: Alex, what happened to your shorts?

  Alex: It was unfortunate. There was an incident. I do not wish to disclose any more details. Things got out of control, and by the way, I am bleeding from my anal fissure again. There is great peril that has happened.

- Alex: Why are you buying sneaky cookies?

  Me: That's because they are for the dogs. They are shaped like bones.

Alex: Yeah, but they have frosting. Gets me every time.

August 2019

- I overhear Alex and his randomness talking to Aubrey:
  Just to let you know, I will call the police if you ever audio or video record me without my permission and consent or if you eat my chicken pasta in the fridge. You wanna break the law, then you're going to jail.

- I am buying some pads for Alex for his bleeding anal fissure. We are in the feminine product aisle. This is a very busy aisle today. Alex announces, "Oh, so all your butts are bleeding too?" Also, after doing some research, he is appalled and disgusted at what they are really buying the pads for.

- Aubrey borrowed Alex's cell phone to call me and tattle on him. Alex is so upset that he was "duped and fooled." It is almost midnight, so I ask them where their dad is.

  Alex: The dad is sleeping, so Aubrey says she is in charge. So here we are.

- We have started practicing staying with Alex staying home alone just for five to ten minutes at a time. Every time, he strips down to his underwear to be "man of the house," and he takes the trash out.

- I have officially legally opened my in-home cosmetic spa. Refresh. Alex says he is my business partner. Don't worry, I will be the only one poking the faces.

September 2019

- Every week, I buy one lottery ticket. Alex is really upset today because I didn't win the Mega Millions. He says I need to try harder.

- Alex held the door open for me and the elderly woman behind me. Such a nice young man until he said, "Come on, let's go. A little faster. I know you are old, but let's get it moving."

- I asked Alex to put his clothes away, and he asked if he could do it tomorrow. I said only if you pinky swear you will do it.

  Alex: I don't understand the context. I don't swear, not even if I hurt my pinky.

- Me: Alex, I think you have some food on your shirt.
  Alex: Well, interestingly enough, it is not food. I sneezed earlier, so it's probably a booger.

- Alex: Princess Mommy, do you know what today is?
  Me: No, what?
  Alex: Today is the day my cousin, Samantha, will have her newborn baby. Everyone is going tomorrow to give the baby a bath. I will be brave and will help birth the baby. I have watched a few videos, and it is gross. But I will do my best.

  He has some confusion about what a baby shower really is, and I don't know why he wants to help birth a baby.

- Alex is having his colonoscopy. The propofol has kicked in, and he is singing to the endo team "A Boy Named Charlie Brown." He also says he loves living in the USA.

- Me: Alex, if I let you go out of town with Dad tomorrow, can you promise me you will be good?
  Alex: Well, actually, no, I cannot promise that I won't be an unruly delinquent.

  At least, he is honest. We are trying to help his separation anxiety from me. He is going to go on a short two-day fishing trip with Nick. I am so glad Nick has patience and is excited to take Alex somewhere without me. Alex loves his dad, but he just shows it differently. It is common that an autistic child will gravitate toward one person. I am Alex's person.

- Alex's translation when he is done with visitors:

  Well, it's time for you to go home. You better get going. You came to visit, and the mission is complete. I am done now with visiting. You should leave my house now and go back to your home. You like it there, and I would like for you to go there. *(Cue him opening the front door and turning on the outside lights)* I see your car is right there for you to drive home in. So it's time to leave because you don't live here.
  Thankfully, my parents are good sports, LOL.

- Alex's popcorn maker has arrived. This week, we are focusing on entrepreneurial skills: Complete with office hours, come get some Botox and popcorn.
  I have the best clients at Refresh and amazing coworkers at Trinity. They are buying up all his popcorn. After he made $100, he closed up and went into retirement. With autism, they will become obsessed with things. Alex now can tell you anything about popcorn. He knows the history of popcorn, every way to make popcorn, and marketing strategies to sell popcorn. Now it is on to the next obsession. He is still obsessed with Legos, of course.

- Alex cleaned my glasses for me. How nice. Unfortunately, he used hair spray.

October 2019

- We got a bulldog and named her Kenzie. Alex does not like her hair. He now says now he will join forces with the German shepherds and be friends. They will have the common goal of getting Kenzie outta here.

- Me: Where are all of my bowls, lids, and silverware?
  Alex: Oh, I throw them away.
  Me: Why? Why would you do that?
  Alex: So I don't have to load/unload the dishwasher.

- I hear Alex yelling at the dogs.

  Me: Alex, what's wrong?
  Alex: The Germans were eyeballing me. I don't like it.
  Me: They have eyes and were looking at you. Is that the problem?
  Alex: Yep, all those eyes looking at me. All four of them.
  Me: But I thought you were trying to be friends with them.
  Alex: Oh, yeah, I forgot. Ugh.

- When Alex needs to desperately FaceTime you, the problem? "Dad is dancing like a Mexican man. He is aye yi ying all over the damn place. He is being disruptive by failing to follow the beat. He is a terrible dancer."

November 2019

- Alex is upset that Nick won't take him to the arcade to play and break the record for *Crossy Road*. He sent me this text: "I am so stressed out by Dad. I really want to go to the arcade, but he would not take me. Now as a direct result, my head hurts, my lungs and heart have internal damage, and I might have developed another hernia. Terrible day for Alex. I will be waiting for you to come home from work. Be prepared because I will be sad."

- The nurse tells Alex to get on the scale and points to an area with an adult and baby scale. Alex starts stripping off his clothes. In between the scales, there was a sign that said Weight with Clothes Off.

- Alex: Princess Mommy, this is a real emergency. Aubrey is trying to kill me. She is attempting first-degree murder.

  Aubrey: I shot him in the neck with a Nerf gun. He didn't die. He is fine.

  Alex: She shot me, and now I have neck trauma. I need a doctor immediately. Tell her she is in trouble.

  Aubrey: Stop being so dramatic. I already said "sorry."

  Alex: Okay, never mind. I'm fine, Princess Mommy.

- Went to the Hibachi Grill. Alex freaked out when the little toy man squirted oil on the onion pile, causing flames. Of course, Alex was sitting directly in front of this. Alex ran through the restaurant to the exit while yelling, "That little Asian man tried to set me on fucking fire. I almost died." Needless to say, we will never be having hibachi with Alex again.

December 2019

- We are in Chicago and not in a very good neighborhood. We were going to CVS, and there was a bus stop right outside. There was about four to five men standing outside at the bus stop—all happened to be African American. Alex ran up to these men and said, "Hi there, my Black brothers, it's me, Alex. Nice to see you." One of the men questioned what he said and did not seem very happy. I immediately told him that Alex has autism and loves everyone. He is not racist and does not mean any disrespect by his comment but that his brother told him that he calls his best friend (who is Black) his Black brother. So Alex thinks he can do the same with every Black friend he comes in contact with. The men started laughing and even gave Alex a high five. So glad we didn't die tonight.

- Alex was invited to have a tea party with Aubrey and me. He declined due to having to wear underwear and pants, and he was upset that Aubrey invited the dogs and toy horses too.

- Me: Alex, my stomach is really upset, so let's have something light for lunch.
  Alex: Okay, no problem, one chili cheese dog with hot peppers coming up. If you don't want yours, then I guess I can eat it.

- Three things today:

    1. I don't know why, but Alex is receiving bow ties in the mail. So he has taken a liking to wearing them.
    2. Alex asked if the new Justin Bieber song "Yummy" is about eating hot wings.
    3. Nick always says he is "ready for some action" when talking about playing billiard tournaments. Alex yelled it throughout the store. He was talking about finding the claw machines. We got many looks.

- Me: Who pooped on the stairs?

Alex: *(Very seriously)* I did not poop on the stairs. Not me. Test it for my DNA. I am potty-trained. It was probably Dad.

Me: Alex, I know it was not you. And no, it's not Dad either.

Alex: I will speak with the Germans. It was probably that Kenzie. I have beef with her.

ALEX AND PRINCESS MOMMY
2020 and 2021

January 2020

- Alex holds the door open at the movie theaters for two women while telling them, "Hurry up, dudes, let's go."

- Alex: I'm going to get into the water fart blaster.
  Me: Have a good time in the hot tub.

  Then all I hear is him giggling because the water is faring so much. Just love him.

- Heading to San Francisco and Sonoma for a few days with the BFF. Alex says he is going to be good for Dad, but there is no guarantee. Tracie has been my best friend since high school. She is my ride or die and has been there for me whenever the kids or I need her. She is my sister for life, and I can't begin to say how much I value and appreciate her. I love her so much.

- I told Alex to put on a nice shirt to go out to dinner in. He chose a *Star Wars* Chewbacca, wearing a Christmas hat T-shirt and bow tie. I pick my battles.

- Saw Nick's cardiologist at the store. He is from Colombia. So Alex said he must be a cocaine and coffee dealer. Cue me dying.

February 2020

- It's been a rough day for Alex. He had a meltdown tonight for hours. He is worried about my upcoming trip to California. He has never been away from me for four days. I am worried, but I know he can do this. And I know his dad and brother will take amazing care of him and comfort him while I am gone.

- I need to say how important it is to have a good support system. I took this diagnosis as a personal mission to help my son to be all he can be. I agree with the diagnosis but definitely not with the prognosis. Finding people who you trust with your special-needs child is a challenge in itself, especially if your child is nonverbal or self-harms.

  My husband, Nick, is the silent behind-the-scenes hero. When Alex has a bad day and needs all my attention, Nick is the MVP. He makes sure the household runs: laundry is done, vacuuming and dishes are done (my personal pet peeve), meals are ready, errands are run, and Aubrey and dogs are taken care of. He is there for anything that Alex or I need. He is the best stay-at-home dad. He cannot work due to his heart condition and is 100 percent service-connected retired.

  My parents have done everything: last-minute babysitter, chauffer to take Alex to therapy and stores, going to school and social events, or running things over for him (like chicken wings). They are amazing with Alex, and we are so lucky to have them.

  My oldest son, Nickolas, is amazing with Alex. If I am not there when Alex has a meltdown, then Nickolas is up. I am so proud of the kind, caring, compassionate, and patient young man he has become. I can rely on him, sometimes a little too much, and he always comes through. Growing up, he would always make sure when his friend's come over that they treated Alex good and did not tolerate anyone making fun of or disrespecting him. He always has been very protective of Alex. And Alex just adores him. It is going to be a hard transition when Nickolas joins the army.

My sister, Lori, has a special bond with Alex. She lived with us when Alex was two to seven years old. While my husband was deployed, she was my rock. She babysat while I was at work and school, picked Alex up from school, and helped with getting him to therapy. She loves him like I love him, and I can trust her with him. I can't tell you how grateful I am to have her.

My absolute best friend, Tracie, is my only friend who I can vent and tell everything to. We have been best friends since high school. I joke and tell my oldest son that "I hope you find yourself a Tracie." It is rare to find someone who loves you for you, flaws and all. I can be myself around her and vent to her about difficult things (including Alex). She listens without judging me. She just listens. She loves my Alex and understands when I have to cancel plans because he needs me.

March 2020

- Every night, we eat dinner as a family. No exceptions. Today, Alex asked if he could eat in the living room. I said "yes," and that we will all eat in the living room. Alex said, "No, I want to eat by myself, not with you, people. I am not wanting to be around people today except for Princess Mommy."

- Lots of appointments today for both Alex and me. So I had to just bring him to my cardiology appointment. In the waiting room, on their television, they have information about cardiac conditions. Alex is now lecturing me about the risk factors for atrial fibrillation, having a heart attack and periodontal disease, and asking what my cholesterol levels are. "Oh, just great, something else for me to worry about with you."

May 2020

- I usually share mostly funny and good times about Alex. But I think it is important to talk about the challenges that autism brings too. It's been a rough couple of weeks. But the last two days have been particularly hard. Alex has been extremely manic, highly anxious, pacing back and forth, screaming violent meltdowns that last for hours, and sleeping very little. This shall pass, and my happy boy will be back. Today, I didn't do much of anything besides hug, snuggle, and reassure my Alex that everything is going to be okay.

- The most perfect quote: "If you got beef with me, it's completely one-sided because I promise you I do not give a single shit."

- On a daily average, Alex tells me that he loves me eighteen times a day. He drives me crazy sometimes, but I wouldn't have it any other way. I am so lucky.

June 2020

- Alex calls holding hands "hand snuggling." When we are out in public, he demands "serious hand snuggles" because he holds my hand to keep me safe from "thugs, danger, cars, and bugs."

- Me: Alex, do you want anything from the Coffee and Pancake House?
  Alex: That's not much selection. I guess, with those choices, I will take pancakes, especially since I am way too young for coffee, and it tastes terrible.

Sometimes, I forget how literal he is.

- Alex loves opening things, which includes removing the label. I never know if I am going to eat a can of soup or green beans for lunch.

- Dinner thought tonight from Alex:

   Grandma always says a prayer before she eats to bless the food so it can turn into poop inside her colon and that it comes out without causing anal fissures, hemorrhoids, or great peril.

- Alex usually hates animals, just not a fan, until he saw Togo at the pet store. He had to have him. He has never connected with an animal like he did with Togo. So we got him. At home, we have three female dogs, and none of them like this male dog. Why? Because even after we got him fixed, he is still a humper. But Alex loves him. Then my dad's dog died. And Alex was sad because his grandpa was sad, which is a *huge* thing for Alex—to have empathy. He said Togo should live at Grandpa's house so that Grandpa would be happy, and he can still see Togo whenever. Togo and Grandpa became best friends.

July 2020

- I was checking out at the grocery store when an older gentleman came up and said how well-behaved my children are. He asked if he could give Aubrey a $2 bill. I said, "Thank you, and that would be fine." Alex then held out his hand and said, "Is there a $2 inside the wallet for a good boy named Alex?"

- Alex: Oh, good, the Cubs are playing again.

Me: Yep.

Alex: I see they are giving Cincinnati an anal beatdown.

Me: What?

Alex: You know, like every year, the Cubs win.

Me: Oh, *annual.*

- Up late with Alex and eating pizza rolls for a snack.

  Alex: Princess Mommy, how do you eat the pizza roll without burning your tongue?

  Me: I let it cool before I eat it.

  Alex: Like every time you eat one?

  Me: Yep.

  Alex: I can't do that because my stomach really wants me to eat it. It may be a conspiracy or something linked to COVID-19. I'm not sure.

  Me: No more watching the news.

- Alex: Why did you not answer the phone in any of the fourteen times I called you?

  Me: Well, maybe I was busy.

  Alex: Busy without me? I don't think so.

- "Anal fissure + the sandy beach = torture that is not for the weak of heart."

  —Alex

- A very old Chihuahua wandered into our backyard. Alex said, "Oh no, it's a Mexican dog. Must be here for Dad." When we called the phone number on the dog's tag, the owner described him as being "old, blind, white, ugly, and has no teeth." Alex laughed because he thought he was trying to describe Dad.

- Alex's new word of the week is *chompable.*

August 2020

- I have been up since 3:00 a.m. with Alex, watching his newest obsession: outer space documentaries. I may die tonight at work. He says I need to stay awake and pay attention to the important information that I am being taught.

- I hear Alex in the bathroom having the following conversation with himself:

   Oh no, what have I done? Things just got out of hand. I mean, I guess it's not that bad. Yeah, it's not as bad as I thought it would be. Maybe no one will notice it.

   This was Alex's reaction to the questionable decision he made to shave off his eyebrows.

- Alex wakes me up from my nap before work today.

   Alex: Princess Mommy, Dad needs medical treatment. He says he is sweating his butt off. It's still there, but he may need help before it falls off.
   Me: Alex, that is an expression. His butt is not going to fall off. He is just really hot.
   Alex *(very irritated)*: well, that's just great. It's like a secret code around here.

September 2020

- Alex was yelling for me while I was in the bathroom.

   Alex: Princess Mommy, I needed you urgently. Why did you not respond immediately?
   Me: Alex, sometimes, I am busy doing other things, and you can wait.
   Alex: Wait, what? Since when?

The reason he needed me was because Kenzie, the bulldog, walked by him and farted. Not sure what exactly I am supposed to do about this.

- Alex asked if he could make himself a little snack. He made a sandwich that had ten pieces of cheese, bacon, ham, salami, roast beef, turkey, pepperoni, jalapenos, banana, peppers, pickles, onions, lettuce, tomato, ranch, and Frank's RedHot sauce. He called it a shaggy sandwich. I made him dismantle the sandwich and eat a normal-sized one.

- I asked Alex to fill up the dog's water bowl. He does this and tells Kenzie, "Don't give me that side eye. And I filled the water bowl for the other dogs and definitely not for you, just so we are clear."

October 2020

- Autism: when you ask a question, you get an honest answer. Like a really honest Alex answer.

  At the store with Alex today:

  Alex *(yells)*: Princess Mommy, you rang up the wrong apples. She rang up red delicious, but she obviously has honey crisp. There is a $2.25 per pound difference. We don't want to get arrested. That was a close one.

- "You smell like melted plastic and old people. Do you mean to smell that way?" This is what Alex asked the Perkins hostess.

- Crappy lungs, asthma flare-ups, and frequent pneumonia have Alex needing some breathing assistance overnight. We arrive and check in at Iowa City.

Woman: What are you checking in for?

Alex: For an overnight adventure with just me and Princess Mommy. We are here to snuggle.

Woman *(looks confused)*: What?

Me: He is here for the sleep study.

- Alex learned how to blow a bubble with his gum yesterday. He also learned a valuable lesson that you do not eat the bubble gum when you are done with it, especially not all fifteen pieces.

November 2020

- Alex drank out of my cup and literally took three huge gulps of straight tequila. Now he is so silly. Mothering fails.

- Alex is watching cow-birthing videos.

  Me: Why are you watching that?

  Alex: Oh, okay, you never know when you may need to assist with a birth. I think a cow and human would be probably the same.

  Alex just watched a video of the calf being pulled out of the mother by a chain and ATV. He asked me, "Princess Mommy, is that how I came out of you?" LOL, no!

- Alex's thought about the COVID-19 swab and how the encounter went:

  I was permanently mentally damaged. I sustained nasal trauma, and now my sniffer is not working right. Definitely would not recommend.

- Alex wasn't feeling good last week, and his asthma had kicked up. We thought it was just his normal asthma exacerbation, but today, we realized something else was going on. Alex is sick with COVID-19 and is being admitted to the PICU at the University of Iowa. He was hypoxic at 87 percent on 3L NC on arrival. We have started the high-flow oxygen, Remdesivir, antibiotics, steroids, convalescent plasma, and IGG infusions. His liver enzymes are elevated, and he has MIS-C. Alex has given us scares before with his asthma and other health problems but never this bad. It is the most helpless feeling in the world to not be able to comfort and make your child feel better. He has no appetite and is weak. Too weak to get out of bed.

- Day 3: Today, Alex turned the corner and has been doing great. We are trying to wean down the high-flow. Today, he ate some Jell-O, which he normally hates. He is watching movies and is in better spirits.

- Day 5: We are off high-flow and now on nasal cannula. He's eating more today and has more energy. He wanted to build the Lego set someone sent him as a gift. He is smiling, laughing, and acting more like his sweet self. He is very angry that they don't have Frank's RedHot sauce and that he cannot taste anything. Alex was very suspicious of the plasma and said it looked a lot like urine. He asked the nurse, "What kind of sick operation are you running here?"

- Day 7: He is continuing to do amazing. Hopefully, he will go home tomorrow. Unfortunately, yesterday, I was admitted to the observation ICU COVID-19 unit. I have COVID-19 and am on BiPAP. I don't remember much of yesterday due to the hypoxia; it all felt like a dream. I am doing better today and just got off the BiPAP. I woke up and was so scared because I didn't know where Alex was or why I was in a hospital bed. The nurse let me know what happened and how sick I was when I came into the ED.

- Day 9: Alex was discharged home today on oxygen. He got home and was freaking out because I wasn't home. Nick purposely did not tell him that I was admitted.

  I decided today to sign myself out. I am doing much better and chose to go home on oxygen. I had the worst roommate, an elderly woman with dementia. Her name was Shcila. She kept yelling at me to get out of her house and to come change her depends. The nursing staff just kept apologizing because there was no other room to switch me into. I understood, and Sheila and I made the best of it. But it was time for me to go home and be with Alex. So the hospitalist agreed to discharge me with medications and home oxygen as long as I signed an AMA for going home too soon. No problem.

  As I walked out, Sheila told me that I better had remember to water her plants and that if they were dead, she was going to kick my ass. She also said I did a terrible job dusting the shelves and that she should never have paid me the $5 for such a shit job. Bye, Sheila!

  I came home the day before Thanksgiving. My husband still made an amazing dinner for us. It was just the five of us, and it was perfect. We sat at the table, Alex and I both on oxygen, and were so grateful to be alive and together. I am not an emotional person and do not cry very often. But that night, I cried like a baby. I was so overwhelmed with happiness that I was home with my husband and children and that everyone was doing well.

December 2020

- Alex's latest favorite thing to do is to ask Alexa ridiculous questions. He is laughing hilariously. I love to hear his laugh. It really is one of the best sounds ever.

- Alex finished a five-thousand-piece Lego masterpiece this morning. It took him thirty-two hours and fifteen minutes of active building. He times himself with every build. Legos make him so happy.

- Alex has a shelf in the fridge dedicated to hot sauces. He calls it the "spicy butthole-massacre shelf."

- What parents of autistic children want you to know:

  1. We save all our patience for our kid. We don't have much left for anyone else.
  2. We are tired but are extremely driven to fight for services and accommodations for our kid.
  3. Never underestimate our kid. They are capable of anything.
  4. The love we have for our child can move mountains.
  5. Life with an autistic child is an awe-filled journey full of ups and downs. Our children teach us about life and makes us a better person.

- Alex called me at work last night for an emergency.

  Alex: Dad said "smell ya later" to me.
  Me: Okay.
  Alex: Why does he want to smell me later? And when will the smelling occur?
  Me: (Explaining to Alex the meaning of the expression.)
  Alex: He better not come into my room later to smell me.
  He then made a sign for his door that says No Smelling Me Allowed.

- When you can't sleep because you are too excited that Santa is coming tonight so you wake your mom up at 4:00 a.m. for snuggles and a Christmas movie. Christmas is so magical and special for Alex. I have tried to tell him that Santa isn't real, but he refuses to believe it.

January 2021

- Mental health often gets an eye roll from people who don't live with it. Is Alex going to die from it? Thankfully, no. But what people don't realize is how utterly crippling and life-altering it can be for that person and their family.

   Alex has just as many mental health days as he does asthma or other health-related issue days per week. Alex does have a lot going on medically in addition to the autism. But when someone is medically ill, you can do things that make them feel better often pretty fast. When he has an asthma flare-up, we start steroids. When he has pneumonia or an infection, we start antibiotics. But it is not like that with mental health. When we start new medications or change dosing, it can take four to six weeks to see improvement. Sometimes, his mania will last weeks with med changes or with major life changes to his routine and life.

   People try to give their unsolicited advice, telling me I need to make time for myself and marriage. My husband and I have a very strong marriage, and we both agree our children are our priority. Or they tell me how Nick can deal with him having a meltdown so I don't need to cancel lunch. Would you be able to just go to lunch with friends while your child is screaming, crying for you, out of control, and/or hurting himself? Well, I cannot and will not. Nick does an amazing job with Alex. But when he needs Princess Mommy, I am there.

   As far as other housing options that people have asked about, the answer is *fuck no*! He will always live here at his home and with his family. This is the safest, calmest, and most loving place for him. There is no shade thrown at the parents who chose to have their child in a long-term facility or group home. I'm sure they are doing what they believe is best for their child.

- Alex: Are Aubrey's earrings real diamonds?
  Me: Why?
  Alex: Because I can use some cash, and I have no more teeth for the tooth fairy. Seems like a good option. I really need to get the Snoopy hot dog bun toaster and ketchup chips.
  Me: I said "no" to the bun toaster. You don't need it.
  Alex: Princess Mommy, but I do need it. I have been suffering with using cold buns all these years.

- Pneumonia again for Alex. Canceling all plans outside of the house today. He just wants Princess Mommy snuggles.

- We went on a big family ice fishing trip for a few days. Alex did so great! He loves ice fishing and even baits his own hook. I was talking, and apparently, I was too loud, so he put his hand to my mouth and said, "Shhhh, the fish can hear you, so you need to be quiet." However, he was terrified that he might have to shit outside.

- Me: Alex, here is your snack bag for the trip. Don't eat them all at once. This is it.

  Twenty minutes later

  Alex: What would happen if someone were to eat all of their car trip snacks? Could that person just get a refill on their snack bag?
  Me: Alex, did you eat all your snacks already?
  Alex: Well, you see...yeah. It's all gone. Wasn't the best decision I have ever made, but it also wasn't the worst. I regret nothing.

- Alex is now venturing into building other things like tables and bookshelves. He is really good and fast at it. His requirements for building are as follows:

    1. Some cash payment
    2. A TV with *The Simpsons* or *Scooby-Doo* playing
    3. Proper toolbox and access to power tools
    4. Plenty of snacks and Frank's RedHot sauce
    5. One regular pop followed by switching to diet pop
    6. No animals to bother him, especially no bulldogs like Kenzie

- Alex is so hungry lately with being on a high dose of steroids and his psych medications.

    Alex: Can I have a snack?
    Me: No, we literally just had dinner.

    Ten minutes later, he brings me a sandwich.

    Alex: Princess Mommy, I brought you a special sandwich that I made just for you. It is a grilled tenderloin with every type of cheese we have, hot sauce, onion, tomato, mac and cheese, and peanut butter. If you don't like it, I know someone who would be nice enough to eat it for you *(points to himself)*.

- Our conversation at 3:00 a.m.:

    Alex: Princess Mommy, I do not like cats at all because they will get your tongue.
    Me: *(Explaining to him what the saying "Cat got your tongue" means.)*

Alex: I don't think so. I'll just continue to hate and avoid cats just to be safe, and I definitely would never let them near my mouth. Never. Not sure what they plan on doing with my tongue, but I don't like it.

Me: Okay, fine.

February 2021

- Watching *The Simpsons* with Alex. He is recording on his phone every time Homer chokes Bart and then sends it to Nick with the message "See what's coming your way."

- "I hope this movie is so funny that you laugh your butthole and kneecaps off."

  —Alex

- Alex at 4:30 a.m.: Princess Mommy, my brain is awake. I did get a full two hours and twenty-seven minutes of sleep last night. I am all ready for my Rhonda-and-me day.

  Me: Awesome, let me sleep for a little bit longer.

  Alex: Okay, I will see you every thirty minutes until you get up. My alarm is set.

- Alex texted me that he has an emergency with Dad.

  Alex: Daddy is being so mean by trying to stare in my direction.

  Me: Alex, come on. Don't be dramatic. Did he happen to look your way?

  Alex: That's exactly what he did. I am not in the mood for this shit today.

- Alex: Princess Mommy, I have an emergency because I hit my arm on the table, and I now have a boner.

  Me: Wait, what? That was your elbow you hit.

Alex: I know. When you have a hard bone that is getting bigger I think it's called a boner.

Me: It's called swelling of your elbow, not a boner.

Alex: Oh, yeah, sorry about that confusion.

- With Alex having a photographic memory, it is impossible to lie to this kid. Like when you tell him we will do something later, that's not good enough. He needs a time and date.

- I am having a quick in-and-out surgery today. Alex tells me, "Princess Mommy, you are so adorable and cute, and I love you. Make sure you don't come home from the hospital with a baby this time." He tells me the same thing every time I go to the hospital for an appointment, surgery, or labs. It happened one time in his life where I went to the hospital and came home with a baby.

March 2021

- The card Alex made for his surgeon: "Thank you for making my butthole beautiful again. We are best friends. I love you."

- Watching *The Simpsons* with Alex while having chips and dip. Alex tells me we are both third shifters. He also says, "Just to let you know, I am going to be an aggressive dipper."

- In case you missed it, Alex is so funny, smart, and sincere. But feelings and empathy he struggles with, and we work really hard on it. So if he tells you that he loves you, then you should feel special. My dad's dog died recently, and Alex said, "I'm sad that Grandpa feels so sad." To say this was a huge breakthrough is an understatement.

- Puerto Rico Adventures:

  1. Visiting the Best Buy and Walmart for his day to pick the activities.
  2. Going to the beach for just twenty minutes followed by strict cover-up protocol to avoid the "torturous sun."
  3. So many inappropriate comments made
  4. Coming all the way to this gorgeous rainforest just to stage a picture of him staging a picture of choking Nick, just like Homer does to Bart.
  5. Eating the island's finest food located only at Burger King and Subway.
  6. Avoiding the iguanas that are everywhere because they were "suspiciously eyeballing me."
  7. Bought a ridiculously expensive canteen because Alex was "dying of thirst," and this way, he wouldn't have to wait for the drink cart on the plane.

- Alex, while going through airport security, says, "Don't worry, I am not a drug smuggler or terrorist. I have no cocaine or weapons." This earns him a pat down. During the pat down, Alex is telling them all about his anal bleeding and Legos. He is quite the conversationalist.

- At the doctor today with Alex. The doctor was checking his throat/neck.

Alex: Oh, are you going to choke me?
Doctor: OMG, no. I would never do that (*as he touches Alex's neck*).
Alex: (*Proceeds to make choking sounds*) why you little…

Me: I'm sorry. He loves *The Simpsons*.

- At Target, I let this elderly woman go ahead of me in line.

  Alex: Did you let her go first because she is very old and rapidly approaching death? I mean, she will probably be dying soon.

  Cue me apologizing and explaining he really didn't mean to be an asshole.

April 2021

- Alex made me a peanut butter and jelly sandwich. I ate it. I ate it all. I came downstairs and saw the fucking dog peanut butter jar on the kitchen counter. Yes, he sure did. He made me a sandwich with the dog peanut butter. *My dogs eat out of this container.* So gross. He said he was sorry about the mix-up on his end. He gave me the dog peanut butter sandwich and then made himself a different sandwich with the nondog peanut butter. He said, "I noticed the mistake, and I don't want to eat after the dogs. That would be very nasty."

- Alex: Princess Mommy, I don't like the blueberries you bought with the sugar on them. They did not taste very good at all.
  Me: I didn't buy any blueberries with sugar on them. That would be mold on the top of the blueberries.

  Alex is now googling benefits and risks of ingesting mold. He says he will let me know if he needs to seek medical treatment at a hospital and may need to call the best doctor he knows (Niki).

- For Alex's big sixteenth birthday, we had a *The Simpsons*–themed birthday party. Alex was Homer, I was Marge, Aubrey was Lisa, and Nick was Bart. Such a fun time everyone had. Alex mingled for about thirty minutes before telling people they should go home.

May 2021

- Alex tells me he loves me on an average of fifteen to twenty times a day. I am so lucky to have him.

- Since having COVID-19 and MIS-C, Alex has been off and on home oxygen and has been diagnosed as a COVID-19 lung long hauler. Alex has had persistent severe asthma and reactive airway disease most of his life. Asthma flare-ups, we are used to it. It is a different kind of hell to watch your child struggle to breathe. But since having COVID-19 last year, it has been difficult to get his asthma under control and to get his PTFs back to his baseline. It has been seven months, and he is still struggling to breathe. He has days that he can't walk more than twenty feet without getting short of breath, days that he tries to swim but can only make it ten minutes before he is wheezing and has to get a breathing treatment. He has days were he hardly gets out of bed because his lungs hurt. Days that he just coughs and hacks, causing fatigue and terrible headaches. We are trying an array of different treatments, medications, and herbals. He was diagnosed with pneumonia last month, and he is still trying to get over it. We are on our second antibiotic and third week of steroids under his pulmonologist's care. The last few days have been miserable for him with all this going on and now with the weather change. So we snuggle, take meds, breathing treatments, oxygen, naps, and watch *The Simpsons*. And listen, anyone who says that COVID-19 isn't real, you can fuck off. You obviously were very lucky you didn't lose anyone you love or have to watch your family member struggle to just breathe.

June 2021

- Alex wakes me up from sleep to tell me, "I just ate a piece of pizza with all the sauces in the fridge. That's just crazy, huh? Crazy like cannibalism. Well, that's gross, illegal, and highly socially discouraged."

- Went to the park with Aubrey. Alex loves playing in the sand, and I let him. But I occasionally run into a douche-bag parent who doesn't want their kid over there with Alex. This is one of those times. I told her Alex had autism and loved playing in the sand. He had every right to be there as did her child. He was just minding his own business. She apologized and said she misjudged the situation. Her child, who was around six years old, sat down next to Alex. Alex told him, "Don't worry, I am a gentle giant. I would never hurt you." They played side by side for about thirty minutes.

- Alex's shenanigans at Mayo Clinic:

  1. He farted very loudly in a jam-packed elevator, announced it, and then asked if I still love him.
  2. He found the Mayo Clinic documentary in the gift shop. It sounded like he won the lottery by his screams of excitement. The lady at the register said she had never seen it and that she had never seen anyone buy it. Alex said to her, "Your loss, this copy is mine. I'm sure this is going to be action-packed." LOL.

3. There was this little three- to four-year-old girl who loves Alex's Grinch T-shirt and was laughing with her mother. Alex said, "The little girl being praised by her mother is a way of positive reinforcement for her preferred behavior just like a dog."

4. During his echo, he was told by the doctor that he was going to put jelly on his chest. Alex asked for grape flavor. He was told it was not edible jelly. He had to try it just in case.

5. I was in the bathroom, and Alex was outside the women's bathroom entrance. Alex was speaking very loudly, "Princess Mommy, what is taking you so long? Are you pooping? I hope you are fresh."

6. In the waiting room, the nurse called for a patient named Bill. Alex started to get up and said he will take Bill's spot instead.

- Alex: So we meet again, my dreaded enemy.

  The man on the escalator was very confused as Alex was talking about riding the escalator.

- Alex can't resist sampling his way through a candy store.

- A Mayo Clinic sculpture is of a naked man. Alex told me to look away.

- I asked Alex to use his inside voice and stop yelling. He said, "You know I'm loud. I don't think I was born with a quiet voice."

- Alex asked me if he could buy something, and I said "no." His response was, "I'll ask you again tomorrow. I hope you have a better attitude then and respond appropriately by saying yes. Let's put our differences aside and come together with your money amount of $290.45 to make my purchase. That does include tax."

- Nick put our American/Mexican flag up. Alex asked if the flag was up because we were having Mexican food for dinner.

July 2021

- Alex opens the door to greet my client. This is his job since he is part silent business partner. The zipper to his pants is down. He says, "Are you here for Princess Mommy or do you want some pizza and to watch *James Bond*?" A fancy, hoity-toity place we are not.

- Babysat for a friend today. Alex went to the garage to get a soda pop.

  Alex: Does he *(the baby)* want one too?
  Me: No, he's a baby.
  Alex: Oh, then does he need like a grape pop with no caffeine?
  Me: No, he is a baby, so they don't drink pop. They drink breast milk or formula.
  Alex: Oh, gross. That's so gross. Glad you don't make me drink that. Also, just checking, he is not ours, right? Like this is not a terrible surprise where we have to keep him?
  Me: Nope, just babysitting.
  Alex: Okay, good. We have enough going on.

- Alex is asking me to thumb-promise him that he can go see *Black Widow* in 3D on Friday. I don't know what that exactly means.

Alex: The thumb is way more important that any of the fingers, especially the pinky. So you have to do what you promise. If you don't, then you will be in so much trouble, like you can be put in jail."

There ya go guys…the thumb-promise.

August 2021

- Alex has the *Star Wars*'s "The Imperial March" song playing on repeat while he is in the bathroom. I knock on the door and ask if everything is okay. He says, "There is great peril with mass casualty and blood loss involving my butthole." He has such a way with words.

- Me: Should we try to eat a vegetarian diet?
  Alex: Why? Am I in trouble? What have I done for you to take my meat away?
  Me: No, you didn't do anything wrong. Just to try something new.
  Alex: Terrible idea. If I'm in trouble, then just take something else away, not my meat.
  Alex *(yelling to Nick)*: Dad, we are in trouble. Princess Mommy is trying to take away our meat. Is this your fault? What did you to do make her so angry?

- Surgery day. Alex had nice, relaxing music playing, Haldol and Versed on board, and his cute blankie. He was ready. He told the nurse, "Thank you for being so sexy and bringing sexy back." I had to explain to him that sexy does not have the same meaning as nice.

- Alex's fortune cookie: "Do not water yourself down to make you more digestible for others."

Alex: What? Why would someone want to spray me with a water hose and eat me?

- I had a rough day today. Alex had made my day instantly better by hearing him say the word *apocalypse*. With his soft palate repair, he cannot pronounce certain sounds together. It literally sounds like he was saying "a cock of dicks." I needed this today.

September 2021

- Alex says he has an old soul, and he picks a new band/ singer from the sixties to nineties to listen to nonstop every month. This month, it has been Lynyrd Skynyrd and The Eagles, last month was Nirvana and The Beatles.

- Went on a riverboat cruise tonight. The captain asked if anyone had any questions about the boat. Alex's one question: When I flush the toilet, does it pump into the river? The water out there looks very suspicious for bodily fluid contamination.

- My best friend got married today! We were so excited. The wedding was beautiful, but Alex got hungry during the pictures.

  Alex: I'm going to forage for food like a bear *(as he eats the grapes off the vine at the winery)*.
  Me: No, Alex stop it.
  Alex *(yells)*: Aunt Tracie wants me to be comfortable, so that's what I'm doing. My belly is hungry and needs food to be comfortable like a bear.

October 2021

- Me to the driver who almost rear-ended me: What an asshat.

  Alex: Why is he wearing a hat on his butt? Do I get an asshat?

  Me: I'll explain later.

  Alex: I can't seem to find one on eBay.

  Me: It's not really a hat you wear. It's just an expression for someone who is doing something stupid.

  Alex: Oh, so do you call Dad that?

- Alex had a soft palate repair years ago, and because of that, he has a hard time pronouncing certain sounds and words. Botox is one of those words, as he says *buttocks*. Alex greets a client at the door and says to come on in for "your buttocks injections." No, no, Alex.

- Alex's random thought of the night: "Princess Mommy, promise me that you will never be pregnant with octuplets. I mean it. I would be so angry."

  I can honestly promise I would never.

November 2021

- Alex left our business, Refresh, a google review:

  I live here with my princess mommy. Bring some money for me too when you come. I like Target, and when you are done, maybe we can go. I also like gift certificates. My house is so much fun. You can use the bathroom since it is fixed now, but don't poop in there, just pee.

  —Alex U.

- I am not having a very good day. Alex reminds me that "At least your butthole isn't bleeding, no one has punched you in the face, and you are not listening to the music of Bruno Mars. So you're okay." This is basically his way of telling me to stop whining like a little bitch.

- The woman in front of us checking out at the store was bitching to the teenage cashier about stupid things like prices of items. Things she had absolutely no control over. Then her card wouldn't work, and of course, it was not her fault for putting the card in backward.

  Cue Alex: "Princess Mommy, I see a Kareen right there. She is doing a lot of complaining and is just not nice. She probably would love to speak to a manager."

  Everyone except for the Kareen laughed. Alex called people a Kareen instead of the typical Karen.
  She looked at me, and I said, "I wouldn't even start with me today."
  She said nothing and turned back around.

- Today was a rough day for Alex. He had a terrible and violent meltdown and knocked himself out when he hit his head on a wall. Now he has post-concussion syndrome. He gets dizzy and nauseous when he stands up and has a wicked headache.

December 2021

- Kias came over for Christmas celebration, and I even got him matching PJs with all the kids. He is such a sweet, kind, and caring young man. He is Nickolas's best friend and is amazing with Alex. He calls/text him weekly, takes him to the movies, and will even come over for dinner and play video games with Alex when he can. Alex loves him like a brother.

- I overhear Alex on the phone: "I am just busy right now. I mean I'm not really busy. I just don't want to talk to you or anyone right now. So don't call me back. Talk to you later but when I call you. I love you. Bye, Grandma."

- My best friend had her beautiful baby, Dylan. I am a god-mother! Alex asked if that meant he was a godcousin, and if so, would he get any monetary present. He was a little disappointed that the doctor did not need his help with delivery. "I was on standby in case the doctor didn't feel well, and if she had explosive diarrhea, I would have stepped in. I mean it doesn't look very hard. The baby pretty much delivers itself. I am confident I can perform a C-section if labor does not progress or if medically indicated. I will watch those videos next."

- Big-boob problem: I burnt my right nipple on the stove while cooking. Ugh. Alex offered to use his medical knowledge to care for the burn, including a hug and kiss. I will take the hug and kiss on the cheek. Thanks, Alex.

- I have shout-out post:

    Shout out to Jersey Mike's!
    I am so proud of Alex as he used his coping skills today out in public to avoid a huge meltdown. We went to eat lunch, and while waiting for our sandwiches, it happened. Bruno Mars's "24K Magic" came on.
    Now this is Alex's most hated artist and song. Again, not sure where the hatred for Bruno Mars comes from. It is an instant trigger for Alex, and something I cannot foresee to avoid when out in public. Alex instantly started scream-

ing and covering his ears. This type of situation can easily get out of control.

We were able to go outside, but the music was playing in the small patio area too. He lied down on the concrete. At this point, I was like "oh, great, concrete with a head banger." But with the help of soft tickles, softly reassuring him that the song would end soon, and breathing techniques, he was able to get up and head back inside once the song was over. People around were staring and whispering in which I didn't give a fuck.

We were paying for our food, and Alex still had his hands over his ears. The manager turned off the music and came over and asked if he could help in any way. I thanked him for being so kind and told him we would just take our food to-go. He compt our food and said that anytime Alex comes in, just call, and he will turn the music off to avoid the possibility of a Bruno Mars song being played. I again told him, "Thank you," but that is not the reality of life. If a Bruno Mars song comes on, we are ready for it.

• Alex is so excited to see Santa. He is so nervous that he might know that he kicked Kenzie for looking at him crazy.

ALEX AND PRINCESS MOMMY
2022 and 2023

January 2022

- Alex's thing right now is the calendar he got for Christmas of dogs pooping.

- "I have decided I am going to be a professional fisherman. I need you to get me fish sticks for dinner tonight. That will be my catch of the day."

- Me trying to explain to Alex what being a "smart-ass" means. His takeaway: "Not only is my brain supersmart because I am a genius but so is my butt. I have achieved the ultimate level of smartness."

- I cut my finger last night on a Botox metal lid. I sutured myself. When Alex saw my finger this morning, he asked if I was involved in an "illegal rumble, fight club, or punched Dad" because those were the only logical reasons for my cut.

- I made a Facebook post about how Aubrey was the employee of the month. Alex was upset and said, "There is only two other people who live in this house. I better be the employee of the month next month."

- I'm not a perfect parent by any means. I feel that my job as a parent is to teach, guide, and support them in being

124

self-sufficient, independent, and a positive contributing member of society. This includes Alex. Some may feel that I push him too much. I want him to be more than his diagnosis.

- "It's just beautiful, absolutely stunning, and has the most amazing dimensions."

  This is how Alex described the pepperoni pizza he just made.

- Alex is selling a few personal items. When Aubrey sells her stuff, she always donates nearly all of it to a charity. Alex would like to make it very clear that all the money he makes will go directly back to him. No sharing of funds here.

February 2022

- Alex farted so loud he scared himself awake.

- Me: Alex, are you being flexible and playing it by ear?
  Alex: Flexible? No. And I am not playing with my ears either.

- My mom is so talented and amazing. She made Alex a new and improved blankie aka cute one. It has some of his old blanket incorporated and fabric that he picked out. It has *The Simpsons*, "I Love My Mommy," *Avengers*, *Star Wars*, autism, and Lego fabric print.

- Alex: What is a normal amount of chili dogs to eat in a sitting?
  Me: One.
  Alex: Oh, well, is it always one? When can it be five?
  Me: No, you can't eat five.
  Alex: Watch me.
  Me: No, it is not a challenge.

Alex: But it can be, and Princess Mommy, I promise I will not vomit. I will hold my vomit in just like a gentleman.

- At the doctor with Alex.

    Doctor: All right, Alex, hop up here on the table and lie on your belly.
    Alex: Oh, like a massage.
    Me: No, it's not a massage. Doctor has to look at your butt.
    Alex: Well, my butthole is nice and clean and ready for whatever this is.
    Doctor: I am just gonna take a quick look at your butt to see if your anal fissure/fistula is back. No massages.
    Alex: Yeah, such a weird guilty pleasure for you, I'm sure.

March 2022

- I'm walking my Botox client to the door when Alex comes downstairs. She says "hi" to Alex and asks how his day is going.

    Alex: It is going pretty good. I just used the newly installed Tushy bidet, and my butthole is spotless. No poop located inside or around the butthole.

    Thankfully she is an ER RN, has kids, and was not in the least bit disturbed by the conversation.

- We went to do an alligator tour, but Alex refused to participate due to being scared that the alligator was going to get me, and then he would have to get wet while saving me.

- Alex is not a fan of salted boiled peanuts. He says they taste like boogers.

- How Alex has been greeting our clients lately:

  1. Sitting on the porch, waiting for his Legos to arrive, and asking if you were a representative from Lego.
  2. Offering you a chili dog while getting your lips done.
  3. Telling you the bathroom by the office is only to pee in, and definitely, under no circumstances, are you to poop in there. Otherwise, Princess Mommy will be angry if you clog it.
  4. Giving you a hug and asking you to take him to Target and pay.
  5. Telling you that he does indeed take and keep tips.
  6. Asking you if you want something to drink. If a client says "yes," then Alex tells her where the closest gas station and gives her his drink order.
  7. Telling you that here at Refresh, "we have the meats."

- Alex is a little dramatic today. Can you guess what Alex is complaining about?

  "This is the worst thing ever. A complete waste of time. I can't believe you are making me do this, and it is against the labor laws. I am completely emotionally upset and may never recover from this monstrosity. Now I have a headache, my belly is hungry, and my foot itches."

  Answer: putting his laundry away.

- Dr. F was made a special "thank you for fixing my butthole three times" blanket. It has butts on it.

  Great job, Mom.

April 2022

- I saw a T-shirt today that said, "Nobody test my gangsta more than my second child." This is the truest statement I have ever heard.

- My new security sign came. It says, "Warning: crazy veteran, bipolar mama, crazy kids, large dogs that bite, and plenty of guns inside. Try me."

- Alex is admitted to the hospital tonight for a post-op infection. Haldol and Versed combination is a wonderful thing for helping him calm down. He just wants to be home. But with a fever and WBC count of twenty-two, he needs to go back to surgery for a wash out/packing and IV antibiotics. My hospital family has been amazing with him. If it's not one thing, it is another. We don't complain because it could always be worse. Last night, Snoop Dogg was playing locally in concert.

  Alex: Did my Dr. F go home because he was too tired from all the Snoopy Dog partying he did at the concert last night?
  Me: No, he went home because it is 8:00 p.m., and he worked all day.

- Conversation with Alex:

  Alex: Princess Mommy, snuggle with me in the bed.
  Me: Alex, I can't. Not gonna happen with that bed.
  Alex: Is it because you are too big?
  Me: Well, it is just a twin bed, and you are not considered petite either.
  Alex: So it's because you are too big.

- Alex is well enough four days later to go home. And he says he is definitely well enough to order Legos.

- Text message Alex sent to Dr. F using my phone while I was driving: It's me, Alex Isaiah Uzelac. I am free after being captured at Trinity since April 22, 2022. I took Princess Mommy's phone because she is driving. You can come to my house and spend the night to play video games and watch *The Simpsons* since the butthole is so beautiful and clean now, and the dreaded butt leaks will stop. Congratulations, you fixed it and made me all better, and I love you. Since we are just best friends, my birthday is tomorrow, so you can come over and bring me a spicy chicken sandwich, and we can go to Target and Best Buy for an epic adventure, and don't tell Princess Mommy because it's like Bro's Code. So I love you and just come over to my house, okay? Don't tell Princess Mommy because I would be in trouble. I am not supposed to text her friends, and my best friend Niki can come too. She is a doctor, but she would not fix my butt-hole and said you can. She is the best. Okay, love you. Bye.

  Me *(really me)*: It's Lynn. OMG, I'm so sorry.
  Dr. F: We are dying, laughing.

  At least his surgeon has a great personality and sense of humor.

- Aubrey is playing by the TV.

  Alex: Aubrey, don't mess around with the TV. It can fall.
  Me: Aubrey, Alex is just worried it is going to fall on you.
    He loves you and doesn't want it to fall on you.
  Alex: No, that's not why. I don't want the TV to fall
    and break because then I would have to watch *The
    Simpsons* tomorrow night on one of the smaller TV
    screens. This one is the largest.

May 2022

- Alex very dramatically stubbed his toe. One of my regular Botox clients said to him that hopefully that was the worst thing that had happened to him today.

  Alex: Well, I did miss the toilet paper when I went to poop this morning, and it went on my hand instead. So there was that.

- Another trip to the hospital and Alex is back home with oxygen. He has pneumonia. Ugh. But he is in great spirits.

- I have cut back at the hospital and have decided to work there part-time. I will be doing Refresh full-time. Alex needs me to be at home as much as I can right now. My kids are my priority.

- Alex's new excuse when he doesn't want to do something:

  I can't. My butthole needs to rest. It is very tired from all the healing it's doing.

- I was commenting on a friend's FB post about toilet paper.

  Me: I can't wait until my children are all out of the house and I can buy the two ply of bougie toilet paper. My kids will clog every fucking toilet otherwise.
  Alex: Princess Mommy, I am here for life, so your butthole will never know that level of ultimate softness.

June 2022

- Today was a rough and love behavioral/hypersensory day. Once the Haldol kicked in, we both were able to finally relax and sleep. Hopefully, tomorrow will be better. For tonight, it is snuggling in princess mommy's bed.

- When going through security, they had to pat Alex down.

    Alex: Is it because I have a boner?
    TSA: No, sir, it's because you have a portable oxygen machine with you. We have to make sure it is not a bomb or weapon.
    Alex: Oh, good. Okay, just be careful where you pat. Please avoid my wiener bush.

- My turn for security. I was walking through the scanner and was not wearing my special airport bra.

    TSA: Hold on. Ma'am, what is inside your shirt?
    Me: What do you mean?
    TSA: There is something heavy on your chest area and around your chest.
    Me: That is just a really good double-wired bra to hold up the boobs. I am not a fan of saggy titties.
    TSA: Oh, okay *(cue Alex who is now through security yelling, waving, and doing thumbs-up signals to me)*.
    TSA: Is he with you?
    Me: Yes.
    TSA: Yeah, I'll need to search you.

- When you are playing video games with your cousin but Grandma keeps interrupting:

    G: Hi, Alex, I love you.
    Alex: Yes, Grandma, of course, you do.
    G: Good. I heard you had a great time.
    Alex: I am challenging Ava, so I have to go. Do not message me again, please.
    G: Okay, good luck.

Alex: Okay, but seriously, I am very busy with an important meeting. Do not type on your phone and hit send to me anymore tonight. I will text you tomorrow maybe. Love you.

July 2022

- Alex went to the neighbor's house the other night to "hang out and chill with Chad." Well, Chad made him a bologna and hot sauce sandwich. Alex says they are best friends.

  Alex: Princess Mommy, when can my best buddy Chad come over to spend the night for an epic sleepover? We will be like party animals and play video games and eat snacks. He will have to ask his mom if he can come over for the sleepover. He can tell her that he will clean his room and be a good boy.
  Me: He is a grown man. He doesn't have to ask his mom, and he can't come over for a sleepover.
  Alex: Then does he need to ask his girlfriend?
  Me: Nope, because he doesn't have a girlfriend. He is married to his wife.
  Alex: I don't know who he has to ask, but he needs to figure it out. And he can stay the night because he is very nice and definitely not a weirdo.

- Another Dr. F text message from me: Hi, there, it's me, Alex Isaiah Uzelac. I have great news that my butthole survived Huntington Beach adventure in California from June 17–23, 2022. The butthole is doing much better and only had a little bit of blood. And I did poop in the ocean, and Princess Mommy was very upset at this, so if you go to the ocean, you need to know that you can only pee in there and definitely not poop, just to let you know. Okay, I love you so much and make sure you can come to my house for an epic sleepover, so ask your mom if you can come over.

Well, pick me up to go to Target or Goodwill for treasure hunting.

Me *(the real me)*: It's Lynn…sorry.
Dr. F: These always make my day.

- Allergy testing with Alex today went well. Here are some tips from him:

    1. The negotiation. Ask for a $800 Lego set when you secretly want the $500 set. This way, Princess Mommy will cave.
    2. Have plenty of lottery tickets to scratch off to pass the time.
    3. Tell the doctor to be careful to not stab you in the heart on accident or on purpose even though the teeny needles are put on the back.
    4. Ask the doctor if she has performed this test before and what her credentials are. Also, inform her that you have researched this test, and then offer to perform the test yourself.
    5. Before the test begins, tell everyone in the room to pray for you. "Rest in peace as this is my inevitable demise by the massive stabbing that is going to take place. Princess Mommy, can we go to McDonald's afterward?"
    6. Once the "mass stabbing" is happening, scream the following phrases superloud and after each of the thirty pokes:
        - Woo-whoo, I'm gonna feel that in the morning.
        - It's nothing but a gangsta party.

- Such a guilty pleasure for you.
- I'm charging extra for that one.
- That's what she said.

Once it is complete, then tell the doctor, "Well, I didn't die, but it was a close one. My heart almost exploded. Thanks, hotshot." And remind her that you will be waiting for your sticker.

- I always tell Alex that your triggers are your responsibility to work on and learn to cope. It isn't the world's obligation to tiptoe around you.

August 2022

- Some days, it is okay to have a lazy day and do nothing. Some days, Alex is too hyperstimulated and requires this. I need to get better at being okay with doing nothing every once in a while.

- Alex was checking in for surgery at the hospital this morning. There was a very pregnant woman who was also checking in at the same time.

Greeter: Are you all together?
Alex: Well, I guess so. We did enter the building at the same time. Princess Mommy, the time has come for me to deliver this baby, I guess *(points at her very pregnant belly).*
Me: No, no, we are not together. And no, Alex, you will not be delivering her baby.
Alex: Okay, yeah, I'm just too busy today. Maybe next time.

All parties involved had a great laugh.

- Me: Alex, can you share that doughnut with me?
  Alex: Do I have to?
  Me: Well, that would be nice.
  Alex: *(ate the entire donut)* no, thanks.

September 2022

- Oh, Dr. F is such a great sport:

  Hi, there, it's me, Alex Isaiah Uzelac, and my butt and violent stab wounds from the mole removal done on August 15, 2022, are healing without death. Thank you so much, and we are best friends, and you can come over to spend the night and hang out, and you have a lot of children, so you can bring one of them. Just pick your favorite one and ask your mom if you can hang out at my house. Princess Mommy will get us snacks, but you can bring some too, and we can have a hot-wing eating challenge, and hopefully, it will not cause great peril to the butthole with the aftermath turmoil from eating the super-hot sauce, and I will see if my best friend Niki can come too so we can go to Target and order Legos, and I have broken my phone, which is so sad, during a terrible meltdown, and don't tell Princess mommy because I am not supposed to contact you outside of the office, but we are like best friends, so it's okay and like Bro Code, so don't tell on me, okay? I love you and ask your mom.

- At my niece's baby shower and Alex put his head to her belly. Alex said he could either feel the fetus kick him or that she was about to have violent diarrhea.

  During the baby shower, I couldn't find Alex for a few minutes. I found him down the hall in the laundry room asking to check the dryer for spare money. Alex said, "It's okay, Princess Mommy, I am just hanging out with my Mexican friends here."

• Alex was so excited that a coworker of mine had mittens made for Alex and me. Now we are watching TV, holding hands, holding very sweaty hands.

• Alex only wanted to order pizza so he could tell the pizza delivery guy to "keep the change, you filthy animal."

• Alex: Princess Mommy, I think you need to call a plumber.
  Me: Why? What happened?
  Alex: Well, someone clogged the toilet by using sixteen
      flushable wipes. Someone then tried to plunge the
      toilet, but that did not work. Then someone put soap
      in the toilet to make it slippery so the wipes and poop
      would just slide down. Sadly, this failed to work. That
      someone also might have accidentally flushed a wash-
      cloth. Just so you know, that's what I think happened.
  Me: It's just you and me here. I think I know who that
      someone is.
  Alex: Was it you?

• What is Alex doing at Lam? He is in his underwear, eating a chili cheese dog, while listening to "Feel Right" on repeat. He says he is just living his best life.

October 2022

• Requirements for Alex to go on a fishing trip without me:

  1. Months of planning the route stops.
  2. Same amount of time researching the local attractions and arcades, weather pattern, history of natural disasters,

Lego store locations, cell phone reception, and fishing reports.

3. Alex's equipment: three inhalers, nebulizer machine, portable oxygen, DVD/Blu-ray players, eight of his top movies, his cute one (aka blankie), and a bag full of random things from home that bring him comfort.

4. Thorough inspection of the lodging accommodations and making sure there is everything physically there that is advertised in the listing.

5. Lots of reassurance that he will be okay and that I will be okay here without him

6. Making sure he will have an adequate amount of snacks and that hot sauce is available.

7. I need to be available to FaceTime, call, and text when he needs me. He told me, "If you need to poop, then just take your phone with you."

8. Reminding him that bait fish are not food.

9. He can use a portable urinal in the boat, but poop is still just for when he's on land.

- Best Halloween shirt I bought: Alex says, "I put a spell on you. Just kidding. It's just the Haldol."

- The weird things Alex says while at the dentist:

  1. Did you wash your hands after you went to the bathroom today?

2. Calm down there with that tooth torture device. Let's not get too out of hand.
3. I'm hemorrhaging from blood loss (he had very little gum bleeding).
4. Princess Mommy, if I get a boner, just know it was not part of the plan.
5. I will need to take this home with me (a little solo cup). Whenever Alex goes to the dentist or doctor, he has to take something from the office home with him. He has a drawer in his room of random items from his appointments.
6. This must be such a guilty pleasure for you, hotshot (while getting his teeth flossed).
7. I am a little disappointed in the sugar-free sucker selection, rating it a harsh 5/10.

• While at a busy social gathering, Alex says, "I think my butthole is very nervous, and there may be a rumble soon." He then lets out the loudest fart I have ever heard.

• Alex: Dad is being an unruly weirdo by using his superzoom eyes and is scope-seeing (when he puts his hands to his face, acting like they are binoculars). Dad is acting like a complete fool.
Me texting Dad: Are you annoying Alex right now by scope-seeing?
Dad: No, I'm just in the living room.
Alex: See attached photo. Proof of the liar Dad as he creeps by my room slowly while having his superzoom eyes in full use.

- Alex has found his new favorite Halloween pastime. It is chasing little kids with a huge remote-controlled spider. I have little kids crying because the spider is chasing them, and then they fall into the baby zombie cemetery. Alex is hilariously laughing, and thankfully, so are the parents.

November 2022

- Princess Mommy, I drank all of your water because you make the best iced water.

- Me: Alex, did you use my toothbrush again?
  Alex: Why? Well, maybe. Okay, yes I did.
  Me: Why won't you just use yours?
  Alex: Why won't you just share?

- Alex loves to text one of his best friends, Chad. Today, here is their conversation:

  Alex: This is Alex Isaiah Uzelac, and I am using Princess Mommy's phone since my phone tragically broke while having a terrible meltdown, and I threw it. It is your birthday today, and you were born a long time ago, probably in the sixties or seventies.
  Chad: I was born in 1974, buddy. So you are right.
  Alex: I know I was right. You are forty-eight years old. What time of the day was your birth? What time did you emerge into the world from your mother?
  Chad: Well, that was a long time ago, Alex. But I do believe it was around 5 something a.m.
  Alex: Were you born by caesarean section or by traditional, painful labor?
  Chad: Painful labor, LOL. But it wasn't painful for me.
  Alex: Oh, I bet you're gonna feel that in the morning. I am making meatballs while Princess Mommy is Botoxing. Do you want a birthday meatball sandwich?

Chad: Well, sure, that sounds great.

Alex: I will bring you one when Daddy gets home. Yes, I know we are best friends, and you are very old now, so I can take care of you.

Chad: Yes, we are best friends, and that's good 'cause I need somebody to take care of me.

Alex: Is your girlfriend Tonya sick of doing it? Princess Mommy is sick of cleaning up after the messy Dad.

Alex then takes Chad a meatball sandwich while in his underwear. Thankfully, we live on a dead-end street, and Chad lives only two houses away.

• Alex made me hot chocolate. How sweet. He handed it to me and accidentally dropped it on my crotch. Now I sit with an ice pack on my cooter and a new fresh cup of hot chocolate.

December 2022

• Alex: I tried the new soap you bought, and it works terrible. I rate it a 0/10.
Me: Which soap?
Alex: It is only for men. It's called Mr. Clean.
Me: Well, that's because it is for cleaning and scrubbing the bathroom. It is not meant for your body.
Alex: Oh, no, what have I done?

• In preparation for our upcoming trip to Jamaica, Alex has been watching the movie *Cool Runnings* on repeat. He also wants to know if we are required to use the "reefer" while there.

- Things Alex does while going through security:

    1. Run like a bull while doing the *Superman* through the security metal detector.
    2. Being told to try again and just walk through the metal detector. Failed again.
    3. Third attempt to just walk like a normal human through the goddamn metal detector. TSA agent laughing and giving up, telling Alex, "All right, then, you do you, babe."
    4. When they powder your hands looking for explosive residue, say, "You won't find any drugs or explosive powder on me. I know the drill."
    5. When being patted down, tell them, "No wiener bush search, please. Be careful of the goodies."
    6. Announcing that you just farted and then explaining how you sometimes have a bloody butthole.
    7. Also announcing that someone's shoes smells terrible, then reassuring everyone not to worry because it is just yours.

- Alex is excited because he was named an honorary Jamaican by one of the nice store owners. Alex said he was excited to be here with all of his Black brothers. I love that he sees no color and just people and love.

- Everyone here in Jamaica fist-bumps. Alex is not a fan and tells people, "Please don't punch me. No punch for me."

January 2023

- Alex was the special guest at the QC Storm hockey game tonight. He even got to ride the Zamboni machine and be on the jumbotron. This is a big deal to him and made his whole week. Thanks again!

- A new client of Refresh came to the door. Alex opened the door and said, "Come on in. I'll be right in to Botox ya." The client had a look of terror followed by relief when I told her that he would in no way be doing any of the Botoxing or any other procedure. He went to make a chili dog.

- How do you milk an almond to get almond milk? There are no nipples.

- Text messages from Alex and Dad:

  Dad: I'm feasting, oh, dear. I'm going to eat all the pork chops because I am so hungry. Don't try to get any.
  Alex: I'm going to tell Princess Mommy, and then she will give you a spanking as a result.
  Dad: Oh, no! Don't tell her, please, no.
  Alex: Oh, I'm telling, mister. You are a bad boy for eating all the pork chops, and Princess Mommy said she will handle it. You are going to get it.

- Alex went on a four-day fishing trip without me. He did *amazing*! I am so proud of him. He has come a long way from only being able to tolerate one day away from me. I love to see him and Nick doing things together, and he loves that Grandpa and Uncle Scotty do too.

- Alex has a new obsession: *Wheel of Fortune*. He solves the puzzle so quickly and then yells at the contestants. He said

Snoop Dog was the dumbest contestant ever. I thought I knew the answer to one of the puzzles. I was wrong. Cue Alex saying, "What? Why would you choose such a dumb answer? It obviously is not right. Come on, now, get it together, Princess Mommy."

February 2023

- On vacation in Colorado, Alex told a lady that he was here for a peep show.

  Me: No, no, you are not. What are you even talking about?
  Alex: You know, a fun, good time.
  Me: No.
  Alex: Yeah, a Lego peep show. I will get a sneak peek of what new Lego I am going to be getting.

- While on the cave tours:

  Me: It smells in here.
  Alex: Oh, no, is it me?
  Me: No, it's all the sulfur.
  Alex: Is that what farts are called when it happens inside the caves?
  Me: No, they are still called farts. Did you fart?
  Alex: Yes, I was nervous because the fart smell wouldn't go away.

- Same cave tour (almost over):

  Guide: Does anyone have any questions?
  Alex: Oh, god, no.
  Me: Alex, stop it. People can ask questions.
  Random lady: *(Puts her hand up.)*
  Alex: Oh, no, don't do it.

Same random lady: *(Asks questions.)*
Alex: *(Stares at her)* you.

- At the store with Alex and we are checking out. The cashier asks Alex how his day is going. Alex says, "Well, I am a boy, so I do not get periods. My day is going pretty good then."

- We have a birdhouse outside, and the "ME" fell off from "HOME." Alex asks me what Ho House birdhouse is. I told him it is because all birds are welcome. Alex says, "Oh, okay, so we are the Uzelac Ho House." No, Alex.

- Alex loves arcades almost as much as Legos. Every Sunday, if Alex has good behavior all week, he gets to go to the arcade. He loves the game *Crossy Road*, and today, he beat the all-time high score. He had staff and a hoard of eight- to nine-year-olds chanting and cheering him on. He was so excited, and everyone in the place heard it. I love seeing him so happy.

- Alex cut his finger, and we only have *Frozen*-character bandages. Cue the meltdown. "Princess Mommy, you cannot expect my wound to be healed by Elsa. I obviously need Yoda to heal this massive hemorrhaging cut." FYI: it was a very small cut and was not even bleeding.

- Alex at 3:00 a.m.: Princess Mommy, wake up. I need to tell you something.
  Me: What is it?
  Alex: I just want you to know that I love you so much.
  Cue my heart melting. But now it is 7:00 a.m., and I still cannot go back to sleep. It's going to be a long day.

March 2023

- Alex learned that while in Target, it is highly frowned upon to shop out of other people's carts.

- At Mayo Clinic with Alex for his yearly cardiac appointment. Alex was told to take his shirt off and put the gown on open to the front. I stepped out to use the bathroom, and the echo tech also stepped out for a minute. We both came back to the room at the same time. He didn't follow directions and stripped down naked. He said, "Oh, sorry about that. There was some confusion, which led to an awkward encounter."

- Alex's preferred method of cutting up vegetables is by karate-chopping them with his hands. I have quite the mess in my kitchen.

WHAT'S NEXT?

I tell ya, this has been such an incredible journey. To watch Alex grow and surpass all expectations and limitations that was part of his initial diagnosis has been so overwhelmingly amazing. And we celebrated every milestone. He is different, unique, intelligent, hilarious, kind, and is my gentle giant. He has no filter and has such a sweet innocence about him. His journey has been filled with laughter, joy, happiness, sadness, frustration, meltdowns, anger, accomplishment, and challenges. But he has faced every obstacle with determination, determined to crush his goals, get Legos, and move onto the next goal. He worked his butt off in therapy for twelve years. He graduated from OT, PT, speech therapy, and behavioral therapy at the age of fourteen years old. We had a big party and celebrated him and all the hard work he put in. It was anything but easy, but he did it.

Thank you to our family and close friends who get Alex and who love him just the way he is. A special shout-out to Alex's siblings, Nickolas and Aubrey, you guys have always treated Alex with respect, love, patience, and kindness. You both help to encourage him to be the best version of himself. I cannot tell you how much your dad and I love you and how proud of both of you we are. And I am a firm believer that you both are such kind and empathetic people because of Alex.

Since high school has been completed, we focus on life skills. He is learning how to pay bills, how to take care of himself (shaving, laundry, grocery shopping, cooking, etc.), how to mow the lawn, and other household jobs. He has chores he does every day here at the house. We tell him, "If you live here, then you help out. Everyone has to do their part." He sometimes gets annoyed and reminds me that "this job is a waste of time, and you should hire a maid to do them." After the brief complaining, he does makes sure his daily jobs of dishes and trash are done. Don't worry, he gets plenty of Legos. He is still a master builder and has his collection insured. He will not be driving as that would not be a safe situation for Alex or others. He will always live at home here with us. This will always be his home. Alex still struggles with sarcasm, jokes, and can be pretty socially awkward. We continue to work on these areas. He requires his blankie aka his cute one for trips and to go to the hospital. This brings him comfort and familiarity. He is still learning to think before he speaks and when it is and is not appropriate to say things. Oddly enough, sometimes, I think our world actually needs more people like this.

A big step for Alex is how well he has been on vacations. Alex has adjusted to vacations and actually looks forward to them. He helps to plan them and to come up with the daily itinerary. He researches the area we are going to and outlines any foreseen dangers of the trip. He has come such a long way from me having to carry him screaming through TSA and them thinking I was abducting a child.

Another big improvement is his increased independence. He is even able to stay home alone for up to an hour or so. Of course, with strict rules of not answering the door or cooking anything in the kitchen.

Alex also has been very active lately in our small business, Refresh Botox and Fillers. He greets clients at the door, will ask them if they would like a snack, ask them if they would like to come in to watch *The Simpsons*, and tell them to have a great day after their appointment. He never ceases to amaze me.

I hope you all have enjoyed learning about Alex and who he really is. He can show love and can be so sweet. His laughter is so infectious. He is wickedly smart. When Alex loves, he loves with his whole heart. Autism does not define him or limit what he can or cannot do. He has proved the medical and school community wrong and did it with such determination. He truly is my gentle giant, and I will always be his princess mommy.

I leave you with his favorite saying to me and to those he loves, "You are adorable and cute, and I love you so much. And I just want you to know that my belly is hungry."

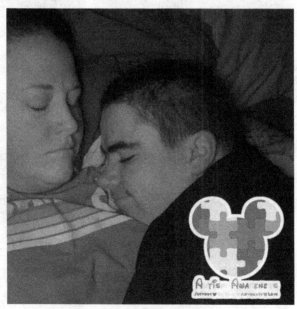

ABOUT THE AUTHOR

Lynn Uzelac is a dedicated mother to her three children, Nickolas (twenty), Alex (eighteen), and Aubrey (nine). She has been married to her husband, Nick, for almost twenty years. She became a registered nurse in 2010. She went to nursing school while having two small children and a deployed husband. She has been practicing as a nurse practitioner for seven years in emergency medicine. She opened her own cosmetic spa in 2019 doing Botox and facial fillers. This is a family business, and Alex loves to be the door greeter. She has three fur babies, two German shepherds and one old English bulldog. She loves spending time with her family, watching the Chicago Cubs, listening to music, and being outdoors. Her favorite place to be is at the beach. That is the place she loves to go to reset and relax.

Printed in the USA
CPSIA information can be obtained
at www.ICGtesting.com
LVHW090022191123
764224LV00063B/2267